Adventist Hot Potatoes

Martin Weber

Pacific Press Publishing Association
Boise, Idaho
Oshawa, Ontario, Canada

Edited by Lincoln E. Steed
Designed by Dennis Ferree
Cover illustration by Sandra Speidel
Typeset in 10/12 Century Schoolbook

Library of Congress Cataloging-in-Publication Data:
Weber, Martin, 1951-
  Adventist hot potatoes / Martin Weber.
     p.   cm.
  ISBN 0-8163-1039-4
  1. Seventh-day Adventists—Doctrines. 2. Adventists—Doctrines.
3. Sabbatarians—Doctrines.   I. Title.
BX6154.W422 1991   91-170
286.7'32—dc20   CIP

91 92 93 94 95 • 5 4 3 2

Contents

Chapter 1

Legalists Versus Liberals

(Our Challenge in the Nineties)

Let's call her Linda. She showed up in church one morning after discovering the Sabbath through Bible studies.

After visiting for several weeks, Linda learned that her commandment-keeping friends were vegetarians. That seemed strange, but saying goodbye to hot dogs and hamburgers posed no problem for such an eager believer. Determined to live up to all new light, Linda went to the ABC and bought a meatless recipe cookbook. Then, stretching her slender food budget, she prepared a large lasagna casserole for fellowship dinner. She could hardly wait for Sabbath to share it with her new church family.

As soon as the service ended, Linda dashed home and took the steaming casserole out of the oven. Returning to church, she carried her dish into the fellowship hall and, with a proud smile, set it on the table.

It was her first attempt at Adventist cooking. It would also be her last.

One of the saints had been keeping a wary eye on Linda since the first Sabbath she attended services. Now this veteran commando of the spiritual SWAT team swung into action. "Don't you know Sister White says eating cheese is unhealthful?" she demanded.

For a moment Linda stood there, stunned. Then, bursting into tears, she grabbed her meatless abomination and fled.

Nobody ever saw Linda at church again.

Lots of sinners will be lost snorting cocaine and sloshing beer. But is it possible that some scrupulous saints will likewise go to hell sipping lukewarm soy milk and munching oil-free tofu-burgers?

"Whoever causes one of these little ones who believe in Me to stumble, it would be better for him if a millstone were hung around his neck, and he were thrown into the sea" (Mark 9:42).[1] Strong language from One who Himself suffered continual attack from the right-wing extremists of His day! How must He feel today when last-generation Pharisees are holding hostage entire churches and sometimes even conferences?

No less a problem than rigid legalism is the opposite extreme, lax liberalism. Thousands of Adventists have become ice cold in their commitment to behavioral standards. All they seem to care about is that everybody is sweet and loving and nobody condemns anybody for anything (except legalism).

Jewelry? Let it all hang down. Movies? Anything goes for these liberated souls. The only forbidden activity on their list of questionable amusements is Ingathering. They regard the principle of Sabbath rest as the skeleton of an ancient dinosaur. They eat just about anything, celebrating their freedom with a toast of California wine.

These Adventist refugees from what they see as stultifying legalism consider our church a nonprophet organization. To them, the big "G" in the name of Ellen G. White represents guilt.

You see the problem. Many Adventists are ensnared in either legalism or liberalism. The complexity of the questions involved forbids an easy escape.

Think about it. Just where do we draw the line between recreation and wreck-creation? What's the balance between the privileges and the imperatives of the gospel? When does health reform become health deform?

Big hot potatoes, all of them. In this book we will take them out of the oven and put them on the table, along with other questions of controversy, such as:

- Are we God's final remnant, or are we Laodicea? Perhaps both?
- Does the Adventist organization enjoy eternal security in a caffeine-free cocoon, "once-saved, always-saved" from the threat of losing favored status with God?
- How have standards legitimately changed since the nineteenth century in areas of adornment, dress, food, and music?
- Is it lawful to eat out on the Sabbath day?
- Will God kill sinners or simply let them reap death as the natural result of sin?
- Should the extremist troublemakers among us be subject to church discipline?
- And then a big one these days: What about celebration worship?

Vital questions, indeed. In these pages we will search for answers.

You may be wondering, What qualifies Martin Weber to attempt this analysis of controversial issues within the Seventh-day Adventist Church? Well, I'm definitely not an accomplished theologian or a social scientist. But in the last twenty years of working for the Lord, I've had opportunity to witness and experience much of what's been happening in the North American church. I've served in conferences large and small, including a regional black conference during the fall and winter of 1971. For a while I belonged to an independent self-supporting institution. I've been a literature evangelist and a conference evangelist. I know what it's like to plant "dark county" companies in Appalachia as well as lead a multistaff church in southern California.

During the last seven years of my work at the Adventist Media Center, I've answered more than 7,000 letters from

Gladventists, Madventists, Badventists, and Sadventists—as well as from nonmembers reacting to our doctrine and life-style. In my travels I've worked in the territories of all but four conferences in the United States, and half the provinces of Canada. Speaking at camp meetings, workers' retreats, and local church revivals, I've had to dig deep and counsel widely to deal with the issues raised. I've never held an administrative post, and that may be one reason pastors and laypeople alike have freely confided their private concerns and questions.

Through the years, there've been times when I plunged into situations attempting to solve problems, only to make them worse. Nevertheless, I believe my motives have been pastoral. Arguments and controversy I hate, yet how can we bury our heads while honest Adventists are confused on issues of importance? We've got to help them. That's why I'm writing this book.

Well-meaning church leaders sometimes try to paper over our problems, pretending they don't exist. This solves nothing. Worse yet, it fosters frustration and alienation. Thank God for the recent trend to permit and even encourage open discussion of controversial issues for the sake of achieving mutual understanding. As long as we press onward in evangelism while debating the issues, we can find unity amid our diversity and finally fulfill our gospel commission.

In handling our big hot potatoes, I've tried to set aside my bias and evenhandedly examine both sides—or the multiple sides—of these complex issues. I hope I'm sensible enough to realize I don't have all the answers.

Please understand that I'm not speaking on behalf of the Seventh-day Adventist Church, the Adventist Media Center, the Pacific Press, or even my wife. What you read here are merely my own opinions, based on my own study of truth. Some of them I hold quite passionately, especially those involving salvation and peace of mind.

You might be curious to know "where I'm coming from." First, I believe that our only claim to salvation is the mercy of God in Christ rather than any merit in our character attainments. Yet I also believe there is never any excuse for fooling around with sin. Yes, I freely confess my weak moments, but I don't dare excuse them lest I lapse into a compromising lifestyle. There is power available in Jesus such that we can live the rest of our lives without indulging in any temptation, however alluring. I need not suffer bondage to any sin, no matter how powerful.

Now, what if I fail to fulfill my potential for Christian growth—am I lost? It might be possible for me to win fifty souls to Christ next year. But suppose I don't measure up, despite my sincere commitment to witness for Christ in daily living? Am I condemned?

Let's not confuse the possibilities of victorious Christian living with the basic requirement of salvation—a faith that exchanges what the world offers for what Jesus offers. My salvation is not measured by my love for God but by His great love for me at Calvary. In appreciation for salvation, and as a result of full heart commitment to Him, sincere Christians will certainly bear fruit for God—but our hope remains built on nothing less than Jesus' blood and righteousness. Our motto from beginning to end, even after the close of probation, must be, "Just as I am, without one plea / But that Thy blood was shed for me."

Here's the sum of what I'm saying: Salvation comes through God's undeserved grace alone, but the grace that saves us cannot bear fruit of disobedience that disgraces our Saviour.

Are you with me so far?

Let's remember that there's room in the Seventh-day Adventist Church for people of differing convictions. Many well-intentioned but misguided zealots among us attempt to remake everyone after their image. They don't understand that we are not a cult that forces all members into absolute agreement on every matter of conscience. Of course, certain indisputable pillars of faith in Christ define us as Adventists: accepting Jesus as Saviour, Lord of the Sabbath, High Priest in heaven's sanctuary, and our soon-coming King. I'm assuming that the reader accepts these fundamentals.[2] Within the corral of these pillars, there is plenty of room for differing convictions. In such matters, the Lord declares, "Let every man be fully persuaded in his own mind" (Romans 14:5, KJV).

One more thing. Let's keep in mind that loving one another is more important than being technically correct. None of us understands it all, so we must always be humble enough to learn new truth from God's Word. In that spirit I invite you to turn the page for a look at celebration worship.

---

1. Texts are taken from the New King James Version unless otherwise noted.

2. If you have any doubts about heaven's 1844 judgment, the final atonement, or the Sabbath, you might want to read my book *Some Call It Heresy*, available at Adventist Book Centers.

Chapter 2

Dare We Celebrate?

(Celebration Worship)

Rock music playing. Bodies swaying. Sermons saying you can do anything you please in the precious name of Jesus.

Is all this happening in Seventh-day Adventist churches? Yes, according to some. Others deny such reports as groundless gossip.

What's really going on? And what is appropriate worship for imperfect people in the presence of a holy God? Does reverence prevent us from celebrating our salvation in the Lord Jesus Christ?

Let's see what the Bible says about celebration worship. Come with me long ago and far away to the banks of the Red Sea. Daylight has just dawned after the dramatic night of the Exodus. The corpses of Egyptian slavedrivers litter the beach, like the residue of a tickertape parade.

God has set His people free! In the joy of that salvation, Moses' sister Miriam leads the women of Israel in a spontaneous seaside celebration service: "Sing to the Lord, for He has triumphed gloriously! The horse and its rider He has thrown into the sea!" (Exodus 15:21).

I think I know some Adventists today who would have been tempted to round up Miriam's celebrants and cast *them* into the sea. These members believe that our worship of God must be

11

quiet and subdued. They have grave concerns about Adventist congregations that presume to celebrate the salvation God provides us.

"This is no time for celebration," they solemnly warn. "We are to weep for the abominations in the church."

Well, certainly we ought to repent of sin personally, and then humbly yet firmly confront open sin in the church family. In this judgment hour we *must* examine our hearts to ensure that we are faithful. But does that mean we can't celebrate the fact that Christ at Calvary conquered the power of sin and is coming soon to rescue us from this world of sin?

Trouble abounds in the world and in the church, just as Jesus predicted: "In the world you will have tribulations." But then He added, "Be of good cheer, I have overcome the world" (John 16:33).

Christ has overcome, so be of good cheer. In other words, let your heart celebrate His great salvation!

We aren't talking about celebrating sin. God forbid. That's what the Israelites did a few weeks after their holy celebration of the Exodus. While Moses visited with God on Mount Sinai, they forgot their great salvation and, in an orgy of indulgence, danced around the golden calf. That was celebration worship too, you know, and we had better beware of such a counterfeit in our day.

Does my happy way of worshiping God let me get soft on sin, lax in my obedience? Do I think it's OK to frolic in the forbidden pleasures of late-night cable TV and still consider myself a Christian? Do I think I can divorce my wife and then take a new girlfriend to a celebration service so we can indulge in the mercies of God? If so, I'm in big trouble. I'm just dancing around the golden calf, to my own damnation.

Ellen White was inspired to deliver a much-needed warning about the importance of promoting repentance and obedience in our worship services. The Adventist Church needs its message ten times more today than when she wrote it:

> The Lord desires His servants today to preach the old gospel doctrine, sorrow for sin, repentance, and confession. We want old-fashioned sermons. . . . The sinner must be labored for, perseveringly, earnestly, wisely,

until he shall see that he is a transgressor of God's law, and shall exercise repentance toward God, and faith toward the Lord Jesus Christ.[1]

Emotion in our worship is like fire. Nevertheless, we need its warmth; without it we freeze to death in unloving formalism. However, it can quickly get out of control, destroying our souls and our churches.

Jesus promoted a balance between reason and emotion in our worship. He said we must "worship in spirit and truth" (John 4:24). "You shall love the Lord your God with *all your heart*, with all your soul, and with *all your mind*. This is the first and great commandment" (Matthew 22:37, 38, emphasis supplied).

God doesn't want our hearts to race ahead of our heads; neither does He want us to deny our emotions. There is nothing wrong with opening our hearts to express fervent public praise for Jesus, as long as we don't use celebration as a substitute for keeping the commandments.

A lot of good things can be misplaced as substitutes for obedience. Even prayer. If you want to flirt with the deacon and still wear a halo around your head, you can pray loud and long in your Sabbath School class. People are impressed, but God is not mocked: "One who turns away his ear from hearing the law, even his prayer shall be an abomination" (Proverbs 28:9).

So something as pure as prayer becomes a curse when it's used as a smokescreen for sin. Actually, anything we do for God can be abused or taken to extreme. Like health reform. I can care so much about the organic bean sprouts I'm buying at the health food store that I fail to notice the poor clerk worried about her sick baby.

The solution to this distortion of health reform or Sabbath keeping is two words in stylebook keeping, or anything else, is not abolishing the activity being abused. Rather, we must bring it into harmony with the commandments of God and the faith of Jesus. That goes as well for any potential perversion of celebration worship.

An interesting question comes to mind here. If it's possible to make something good in itself, like celebration worship, a substitute for keeping the commandments, can we go to the other extreme? Can we make commandment keeping a substitute for celebrating God's salvation?

Consider the Pharisees of Christ's day who murdered the Messiah in the name of Moses. They were impeccably scrupulous regarding the commandments. Why, they wouldn't even carry a handkerchief on the Sabbath! That would be bearing a burden, you see. So they pinned their hankies to their robes within reach of their nostrils. Unfortunately, their souls were stuffed up with legalism, unable to breathe the fresh air of salvation.

We see them outside Jerusalem on Christ's day of triumphal procession. The humble Galilean has accepted His role as successor to David's throne, riding in royalty toward the temple. His jubilant followers are raising their hands in victory, shouting, "Hosanna to the Son of David, our Messiah." Leading the parade are the children, waving olive branches.

Jesus is Lord! What a theme for celebration.

The religious authorities don't think so. A delegation of dour-faced Pharisees toils up the Mount of Olives to confront the royal procession. They demand that the celebration worship of Jesus Christ cease immediately.

"Impossible!" the Lord replies. "You can't stop My people from celebrating. Why, if they kept quiet, the very stones would cry out in praise of My salvation."

The lesson for us is clear: In the heart where Jesus is Lord, you can't quench the spirit of holy celebration.

I've noticed that some Adventists who oppose celebration worship have no objection to celebrating secular things, like ballgames. One friend of mine warns people against exuberant worship experiences—yet this good brother gets so excited during Washington Redskins football games that people nearby can't even communicate with him.

Seems strange. The Redskins score a touchdown, and 50,000 sportsaholics raise their arms, clap their hands, jump and shout for joy. That's supposed to be OK. But you had better sit stone still in church while heaven rejoices over sinners responding to an altar call.

A fascinating example of celebration worship was the 1990 General Conference session in Indianapolis. Some delegates erupted in appreciative applause whenever the Lord brought them an inspiring song or point in a sermon; others sat in silence. A man next to me leaned over and complained, "It's getting worse and worse, this clapping business. I wish the leaders up front would put a stop to it!"

Stop celebrating Jesus Christ? Impossible! If the Adventist Church won't celebrate, the stones around us will cry out.

I got to thinking. Suppose I return to the Hoosier Dome (where the General Conference session was held) during the football season. I could raise my hands and shout for joy when some man with a helmet kicks a forty-yard field goal. But if I'm hearing a sermon about Jesus traveling more than forty trillion miles to bring me salvation, I'm supposed to stay as quiet as a dead mouse (except for murmuring an occasional lukewarm Amen).

I'm wondering. Is it possible that, when it comes right down to it, heavenly things aren't as exciting to some of us as earthly things? Maybe we celebrate with sports more than with salvation because we spend more time watching the Giants and the Dodgers than we invest in Bible study and prayer. We manage to maintain a form of godliness without the power. Like the Pharisees of old, do we honor God with our lips while our hearts are far from Him?

Often we are just afraid of becoming irreverent. Better not get too happy in Jesus lest we share the fate of Uzzah, the Old Testament man struck dead while "celebrating before the Lord" (2 Samuel 6:5, NASB). The occasion, you may recall, was the return of the holy ark of the covenant from Philistine captivity. As the ark swayed as if to fall, Uzzah impulsively reached out to steady it and was instantly killed by the Lord.

"The anger of the Lord burned against Uzzah, and God struck him down there for his irreverence; and he died" (2 Samuel 6:7, NASB).

What is the lesson about reverence to be learned from Uzzah's fate? How did David behave after several months of heart-searching and self-examination when he finally brought home the ark? Had God taught him to temper his spirit of celebration?

"David went and brought up the ark of God . . . dancing before the Lord with all his might" (verses 12-14).

Can you picture David celebrating with all the vigor he could muster? And the Lord didn't reprimand him for irreverence. Somebody else did. David's own wife took offense at his celebration worship:

"Michal the daughter of Saul looked out of the window and saw King David leaping and dancing before the Lord; and she despised him in her heart" (verse 16).

How undignified and irreverent for the leader of God's people to show such unrestrained praise! And what a tongue-lashing she had waiting for the king when he came home. She even accused him of appearing immoral in his enthusiastic celebration. But David refused to be intimidated:

"It was before the Lord, who chose me . . . . I will celebrate before the Lord" (verse 21).

When somebody really loves the Lord and rejoices in His salvation, you simply cannot suffocate the spirit of celebration.

Obviously Uzzah's irreverence was not the gleeful celebration of God's salvation. What did he do wrong, then? Follow this carefully: His fatal presumption lay in approaching the ark containing the holy law without the benefit of a mediator. Only the high priest was worthy to do that.

Do you see it? The ultimate irreverence is to imagine that we are worthy of access to God on the basis of our own righteousness rather than through the blood atonement of our High Priest, Jesus Christ.

That's something to really think about. Something dramatically different from what we often hear about irreverence.

I found several texts that connect reverence, the fear of God, with the confidence we have in His mercy:

"Behold, the eye of the Lord is on those who fear Him, on those who hope in His mercy" (Psalm 33:18).

"In the fear of the Lord there is strong confidence, and His children will have a place of refuge" (Proverbs 14:26).

"For you did not receive the spirit of bondage again to fear, but you received the Spirit of adoption by whom we cry out, 'Abba, Father' " (Romans 8:15).

So a proper fear of God leaves us confident of our acceptance and adoption in Jesus Christ. That doesn't make us lax on sin: "The fear of the Lord is to hate evil" (Proverbs 8:13). We respect (fear) His holiness enough to repent of evildoing and live by faith in Jesus Christ. His mercy means so much to us that we forsake a lifestyle of sin.

Salvation through God's mercy, not our merit, requires that we meet with Him at Calvary, not at Sinai:

> You have not come to the mountain that may be touched [Sinai] and that burned with fire, and to blackness and darkness and tempest, and the sound of a trumpet and the voice of words, so that those who heard it begged that the word should not be spoken to them anymore. (. . . And so terrifying was the sight that Moses said, *"I am exceedingly afraid* and trembling.") But you have come to Mount Zion and to the city of the living God, the heavenly Jerusalem . . . to Jesus the Mediator of the new covenant, and to the blood of sprinkling (Hebrews 12:18-24).

Do you see the difference between old covenant cringing and new convenant confidence? Unworthy though we may be, we approach God boldly through the blood of Jesus. Any worship or obedience based on fear and trembling stems from old covenant legalism.

Sometimes we urge reverence upon our children by reminding them that Catholic boys and girls keep perfectly quiet in church. We seem to miss the connection between Rome's requirement of absolute silence and its understanding of the gospel. Respect for God's house is essential, but Rome tends to turn reverence into fright, something like the feeling people get in a graveyard at midnight. The only difference is that instead of being afraid of ghosts, many are afraid of God—a God who might get angry when you turn around in church and ask the lady in the pew behind you if her mother is out of the hospital yet.

This concept of reverence says, "Keep to yourself in the house of God. You are climbing the steep stairs of perfection, hoping to be good enough someday to go to heaven. With your eternal destiny hanging in the balance of purgatory's uncertainty, you dare not rejoice in the presence of God Almighty."

Tell me, please. Do you think that some of us need to come out of Babylon's legalistic reluctance to celebrate salvation in Christ? Think about it. If we are uncertain about our salvation, what in the world do we have to celebrate?

You see, beneath all the controversy about celebration worship lies the bottom-line question: On what basis do we approach God? How can we unworthy sinners falling short of perfection relate to the holy judge of all the earth?

If we have any doubt about our acceptance with God, we had better be cautious in His presence, wary of dying in the dust with Uzzah. But if we know He accepts repenting sinners through Christ despite human shortcomings, we can rejoice before His throne of grace. We stand clean before the Lord as His adopted sons and daughters. That's something to be happy about.

Something to celebrate!

Recently I discussed these things with a conference president who has a celebration church in his territory. The music isn't quite his style, and he regrets the occasional anti-establishment remark from people on the platform, but he defends the pastor's sermons as being genuinely biblical and soundly Adventist in content. He resents the exaggerated, even slanderous reports, that have been circulating.

We ought to thank God for the trend toward celebration in the Seventh-day Adventist Church—although I don't think we can automatically put the Good Housekeeping seal of approval on everything that makes for happy worship. But as far as I can tell, the reports of bodies swaying in hypnotic cadence—with sexual overtones—are absolutely false.

We must, beware of the temptation to condemn those whose worship style differs from our own. We don't all have to adore God the same way. For one thing, we have different personalities. Some are quite emotional about their salvation, while others who equally appreciate Calvary are peacefully reflective.

That's an important point for celebration Adventists to remember. Just because someone doesn't enjoy clapping his hands doesn't mean he doesn't know the joy of the Lord. Or just because someone prefers quiet music doesn't mean she doesn't celebrate Christ's salvation in her own subdued way. Some of the happiest Christians I know would not think of raising their hands or clapping, yet they have the joy of the Lord just the same—and their life of uncompromised obedience testifies more eloquently for their faith than the loudest celebration ever could.

Besides one's personality, another major factor in worship style is cultural heritage. A friend of mine is pastor of a church in Hawaii. His Hawaiian and Samoan members enjoy their unique brand of celebration music, while the Filipinos there generally prefer muted praise. Is one culture inherently better than the others?

In mainland America, our black believers have always been enthusiastic in their music and preaching. One of their General Conference leaders told me with a smile, "I don't understand all this commotion about celebration worship. We've always worshiped that way."

It may be that the style of worship typical of black churches comes closest to the biblical model. They bring to God their hearts as well as their minds. When I attend their services, I find myself refreshed as well as enlightened.

Besides cultural customs, another factor that influences worship is the mood we are in. Notice the Psalms. Some are sad or downright mad, others are quiet and contemplative. Then there are many psalms of joy, such as Psalms 149 and 150, which call for jubilant celebration with loud and lively music.

Music in worship must include celebration—but also go beyond it. There's an important place for quiet and contemplative singing, such as after prayer. And sermon appeals call for songs of commitment. I'm afraid that some churches (not necessarily ones I'm acquainted with) could become so caught up in celebration that they have no room for contemplation and commitment.

Pride, selfishness, and rebellion lurk within the human heart, yours as well as mine. Maybe some who seem compelled to flaunt their clapping and celebrating are refugees from the "do-your-own-thing" sixties. Their attitude seems to be, "Just try and stop me from celebrating, you old legalist!" In some cases, perhaps, the "love yourself" mentality of the current age makes a few of the celebration Adventists put more emphasis on personal fulfillment than on faithfulness.

I don't know. You and I can't judge.

One thing is certain, we need a balanced blend of celebration, contemplation, and commitment. Black music usually offers this harmony of moods by mingling soul-searching spirituals with celebration songs.

What should be the prevailing mood of Sabbath worship? Notice what we find in Psalm 92, the designated psalm for the Sabbath:

It is good to give thanks to the Lord, and to sing praises to Your name, O Most High . . . on an instrument of ten strings, on the lute, and on the harp, with harmonious sound. For You, Lord, have made me glad through Your work; I will triumph in the works of Your hands (verses 1-4).

The New English Bible translates that last verse: "Thy acts, O Lord, fill me with exultation; I shout in triumph at Thy mighty deeds." Obviously, God wants our Sabbath services to be a celebration of the great things He has done for us.

Let's sum up what we have so far. Our worship needs a balance of celebration, contemplation, and commitment. And whether we realize it or not, musical tastes reflect our personality, culture, and mood.

To a large degree, worship style also reflects one's age.

Often adults impose upon youth a geriatric concept of spiritual things. I remember when my son, Steve, was about four years old, and I was showing him a picture of heaven in the *Bible Stories*. "Daddy," he interrupted, greatly perplexed. "Is Jesus going to make all us boys wear those big white robes in heaven? How are we going to climb the tree of life?"

A practical observation, certainly. I assured the little fellow that Jesus would let the boys in heaven wear some type of celestial jeans. In fact, the Lord Himself might even enjoy climbing trees with them.

Do you think that's irreverent—our Lord climbing trees with the children? They think it's wonderful. They can relate to a God who understands what makes them happy.

Kids crave activity. Burned-out adults portray heaven as a land of rest, but resting is the last thing young people want to do. And since they don't suffer from our arthritis, let's quit trying to rub our Ben-Gay on them!

Yes, young people need action; that's the way God made them. So they enjoy action-oriented music (in case you haven't noticed). If we withhold from them lively music they can enjoy, the devil is quite happy to supply a counterfeit.

Please remember, I'm not endorsing everything that goes out under the name of contemporary Christian music. Certainly not! Some of what I hear seems cheap, both in words and in sound—and worse, even spiritually destructive. But equally damaging to our teenagers is the kind of Christian music that can bore them to death spiritually.

My daughter tells me that dreary music is the biggest stumbling block to her peers' participation in religion. What a tragedy when our school choirs have to sing only songs from ages past, sometimes even laced with Latin words. How medieval can we get? A preponderance of such music can make our youth see religion as outdated and irrelevant. Some Adventist schools are finally letting their choirs sing contemporary songs, and you can just see the joy in the faces of the youth.

My home church in Thousand Oaks, California, has

adopted a celebration-style Friday night program. Teenagers flock to church on their own initiative for that extra service.

"I'm not impressed," someone objects. "They come because you offer worldly music. You shouldn't pander to the world in order to attract a crowd."

Wait a minute. Our celebration songs are not from the world but directly from the Psalms—the Holy Bible. Is it not the height of arrogance and irreverence to consider songs in a hymnal, which we produced, as superior to celebration Psalms, which God inspired?

One editor of an independent publication gravely observed, "Do you know why celebration pastors put up the words of songs on the overhead projector? That way their hands can be free to raise in the air and clap with."

Well, what's wrong with that? Notice what the Bible says: "Oh, clap your hands, all peoples! Shout to God with the voice of triumph" (Psalm 47:1).

God's Word says we can clap our hands and joyfully voice our praise as we worship Him together. And here's something else to ponder—something truly incredible. Every Adventist is quite acquainted with 1 Timothy 2:9, which warns women against adornment. But we overlook the previous verse, which says: "I desire that the men pray everywhere, *lifting up holy hands*" (verse 8, emphasis supplied).

Can you imagine that! We take Paul's counsel to women and make it the Magna Carta of church standards—but we totally ignore what the men are supposed to do. Worse yet, we condemn those who attempt to obey God's Word by raising their hands in prayer.

Talk about selective obedience! Folks, we've got a problem here! What gives us the right to reject biblical methods of praise and prayer?

Of course, the Bible also requires us to conduct everything decently and in order. Thoughtless madness and confusion are forbidden, since we worship the Lord with the mind as well as the heart. We must avoid the Pentecostal excesses of some fellow Christians who treasure joy and love as proof of the Spirit's indwelling, yet overlook the fact that true love requires a life in harmony with the law. "This is the love of God, that we keep His commandments" (1 John 5:3).

When I was an evangelist, charismatics would crowd the front seats at my meetings and praise the Lord ever so fervently. But when testing truth confronted their consciences, they often rejected it. Perhaps they worshiped a Jesus of their own creation—not the Lord of the Sabbath. Was their celebration an exercise in emotional fulfillment rather than an expression of true worship?

Only the Lord knows; we must not judge fellow Christians. Many charismatics do have a genuine commitment to obey God—but does that place them beyond deception? Remember that the disciples of Jesus sincerely misunderstood the working of divine miracles when they wanted to call down fire from heaven. Jesus warned, "You do not know what manner of spirit you are of " (Luke 9:55).

Here were true-blue disciples of Christ who did not discern what spirit was leading them to abuse a spiritual gift. It should not surprise us, then, that evil spirits today confuse millions who are seeking for the Spirit's baptism through speaking in tongues.

The Pentecostal-Charismatic movement of this century represents a major backsliding from the gospel of the Reformation. Those who speak in "tongues" focus upon what they think the Holy Spirit is doing *within* them more than upon what Christ at Calvary won *for* them. Putting our trust in Calvary's cross protects us from making a saviour out of our Spirit-filled experience.

Ten years ago a movement swept through our church that emphasized the cross. Unfortunately, there were some who minimized the importance of Spirit-filled living. Today we are in danger of emphasizing Spirit-filled living to the point of diluting our appreciation of the cross. And this could lead to all kinds of spiritual problems.

Some of our members seeking a Spirit-filled experience will probably wander into Pentecostal fanaticism. They may start speaking in demonic tongues. That would be tragic indeed, but does it mean we should shy away from celebrating our salvation? Not at all! Just because the people next door let the fire get out of control and their house burns down, does that mean we should go to the opposite extreme and freeze to death? If we Adventists aren't careful, we can become frozen in formalism like the ancient Pharisees.

Here's a test question: Do you consider it essential to fold your hands and close your eyes when praying? If so, where do we find that rule in the Bible? How strange that we can condemn the raising of hands in prayer and require the folding of hands. If we enforce such traditions as if they were law, are we not guilty of teaching for doctrines the commandments of men?

Certainly it's not wrong to fold our hands and close our eyes in prayer. But to enforce such tradition upon the church—that's wrong. Wouldn't you say?

So let's keep that vital balance, worshiping the Lord in Spirit as well as in truth. Celebration worship without a call to commitment is like warm soda pop froth running down the sides of a styrofoam cup. We need warmth in our hearts—let's just keep it under control in obedience to God's commandments. Then we will be secure against destruction by the demons that inspire both fanaticism's flames and formalism's freeze.

---

1. Ellen White, *Selected Messages,* book 2, p. 19.

Chapter 3

Salvation on Standby

(Assurance of Salvation)

A gold card in my wallet is one of my treasured possessions. No, not a credit card. It can buy nothing and it cost nothing. This special card is a gift from Continental Airlines because I fly so many miles with them. When I step up to the airport counter and check in with my supersaver ticket, I just show that gold card. The agent smiles and upgrades me to first class, free of charge (if space is available, which it usually is).

So here I am at the airport lounge, waiting to board my plane. I've got a reservation assured for seat 2A, and I'm looking forward to a nice flight home. Limitless legroom, big leather seats, and a luscious platter of fruit that Adam himself could almost envy. I may even get to witness to some sports or entertainment celebrity. Someone outside my usual circle of outreach.

All this is quite exciting. You can understand why I feel like celebrating.

Not everyone here in the airport waiting room shares my enthusiasm. I feel especially sorry for the people on standby. There they are, pacing back and forth on the maroon carpet, lacking the assurance of a reservation. No doubt some of them are earnestly praying as they wring their hands in uncertainty. Without the assurance of getting on board, they wouldn't want to celebrate with me. Really, what do they have to celebrate?

I suppose you can guess where I'm headed with my story, so I'll just go ahead and ask the big question. Tell me, if you don't mind—Are you on standby regarding your salvation?

Perhaps you hope that if you can be good enough (in Christ's strength, of course), you might make it on board the trip to heaven. You have a fairly good chance, but no assurance of anything. So you "reverently" wait and pray. Meanwhile, those who enjoy first-class assurance in Christ are celebrating their salvation.

Anytime Adventists discuss the possibility of knowing we are saved, you have a hot potato on the table. Unbelievers in assurance invariably quote a warning from Ellen White, such as this from *Christ's Object Lessons*: "Those who accept the Saviour . . . should never be taught to say or to feel that they are saved."[1]

An alarming statement indeed. Those who quote it seem to overlook its context: "Never can we safely put confidence *in self*, or feel, this side of heaven, that we are secure against temptation."[2] Properly understood, there is nothing here to snuff out confidence *in Christ*.

Notice another statement from Ellen White, often overlooked.

> We are not to look within for evidence of our acceptance of God. We shall find there nothing but that which will discourage us. Our only hope is in "looking unto Jesus the Author and Finisher of our faith." There is everything in Him to inspire with hope, with faith, and with courage. He is our righteousness, our consolation and rejoicing. . . . As we rely upon His merits we shall find rest and peace and joy.[3]

How can we imagine that God wants His sincere children to live in doubt and uncertainty? A supposed hope, and nothing more, can prove our ruin. Each of us must settle it for ourselves once and for all: Is the assurance of salvation nothing but a questionable amusement, or is it a necessary ingredient of Christian faith?

As a young pastor, I suffered a run-in with a veteran member about whether we can know we are saved. Disappointed in one of my sermons, he wasted no time getting to the point:

"This business of knowing we are saved—I don't think it's possible," he warned me. Then he tossed out a challenge: "You show me the receipt from heaven's Book of Life, and I'll believe I'm saved when I see it."

"Fair enough," I responded. "Let's open our Bibles, and we'll find your receipt right here in 1 John 5:1-13: "This is the testimony: that God has given us eternal life, and this life is in His Son. *He who has the Son has life*: he who does not have the Son of God does not have life. These things I have written to you who believe in the name of the Son of God, that you may *know* that you have eternal life" (emphasis supplied).

Well, there it was in black and white, the good news that we can know we are saved in Christ. Unfortunately, that poor unbeliever managed to cling to his doubts. He found it easier to hide inside his old cocoon of insecurity than to venture forth into the promised land of faith in Jesus.

Spiritual security is an essential element of the abundant life Jesus promised. It comes with some conditions, though. Jesus declared: "Not everyone who says to Me, 'Lord, Lord,' shall enter the kingdom of heaven, but he who does the will of my Father in heaven" (Matthew 7:21).

Let me tell you about a young couple whose wedding I performed. When Mike met Cindy[4] he already had several girlfriends—more like five superficial sweethearts, as I recall. Cindy soon became his favorite. That wasn't good enough for them to get married, however. Mike had to bid farewell to the others before he could claim Cindy as his wife. All of them had to go. "So likewise," Jesus said, "whoever of you does not forsake all that he has cannot be My disciple" (Luke 14:33).

No doubt about it. Saving faith involves much more than falling in love with Jesus. Trace the words *faith* and *believe* through the New Testament, and you find both have the same meaning—complete commitment to Jesus as Saviour and Lord of our lives. Faith receives God's gift of Jesus in place of any counterfeit the world offers.

Suppose now that I've found salvation in Jesus. What am I going to do with the rest of my time on earth? Do I dare choose a lifestyle of indulgence in the same sins that put Christ on the cross? God forbid! He wants me to "walk in newness of life," to reflect His unselfish love to a lost and lonely world.

No act of love is more essential than forgiving those who sin against us. In December of 1986 a drunken driver going east in the westbound lanes of the Ventura Freeway nearly killed my two children and me. I managed to avoid his swerving truck, but he hit a car behind me head-on and sent a family of four into eternity.

The next summer in court, the defense attorney tried to discredit my testimony. His client had survived other drunk-driving incidents and perhaps thought he could escape the penalty of his crime this time as well. Well, at first I didn't have much love for that killer. Then the warning of Jesus came to mind: "If you do not forgive men their trespasses, neither will your Father forgive your trespasses" (Matthew 6:15). In other words, we can't expect to be saved unless we are willing to shove aside our resentment and pass along God's forgiveness to those who sinned against us. So I consider it my responsibility and privilege to find some way to convey the Lord's forgiveness and mine to that drunk driver, now in prison for second-degree murder.

At first it may seem that Christ is adding some new condition to salvation by telling us we *must* forgive others if we expect to be forgiven ourselves. When we think it through, however, there's no contradiction in what the Bible says about salvation as a gift. Faith in Jesus remains our only hope, faith that shuns human worthiness and trusts God's mercy. But when we refuse to forgive others, don't we reveal a disrespect for mercy—the very mercy that forgives us?

So I don't earn salvation by forgiving people; I only share what God has given me. If I don't have any mercy in my heart, I obviously have never accepted God's terms of saving my own soul.

This saving mercy of God stimulates the cooperation and obedience of true believers. "We love Him because He first loved us" (1 John 4:19). Now, what does it mean to love the Lord? "This is the love of God, that we keep His commandments. And His commandments are not burdensome" (1 John 5:3).

Without doubt, a life of faith will be drawn into harmony with the Ten Commandments. We still fall far short of God's glorious ideal, certainly, but no sincere believers need worry about failure. "There is therefore now no condemnation for those who are in Christ Jesus" (Romans 8:1).

No condemnation! How wonderful to be forgiven fully and freely in the Lord Jesus Christ. But while forgiveness is unreserved, it is not unconditional. You may recall the parable Jesus told about the unjust servant. His master had set him free from a huge debt, yet the ungrateful man refused to pass along that forgiveness. He went out and hunted down someone who owed him a pittance, threatening to strangle the poor debtor. What happened? The unforgiving servant had his own forgiveness cancelled (see Matthew 18:22-35).

So it is with us. Once forgiven, we must continue accepting Christ's terms of salvation. If we return to our old lifestyle, we squander our salvation.

Let's go back to Mike and Cindy, our young married couple. They are still happy together, and it will stay that way as long as they guard the love they share. Nobody in the world can rob them of their relationship, but they can forfeit it themselves by their own free choice. The national divorce rate tragically attests that there's no such thing as once married, always married.

We Christians, likewise, must preserve our relationship with Christ throughout life. God will keep us in His grace, but only as we continue yielding ourselves to Him. He never forces us to follow Him against our will, either before or after we become Christians.

Well, if it's possible to become lost again once we have been saved, at what point would we forfeit our salvation? Many conscientious believers fear themselves bound for hell every time they yield to some momentary temptation. They actually think they are lost and saved again a dozen times a day as they sin and then confess some failure.

Certainly Christians must confess their shortcomings. The Bible says, "If we confess our sins, God is faithful and just to forgive us our sins, and to cleanse us from all unrighteousness" (1 John 1:9). But does this mean God withdraws forgiveness when we sin until we make confession?

Not at all. Notice that the verse we just read is sandwiched between two warnings about *refusing to admit* our sinfulness. Verse 8 cautions that "if we say that we have no sin, we deceive ourselves." Then verse 10 says that if we deny our sinfulness, we make God out to be a liar. Every inspired warning against unconfessed sin involves sin we refuse to confess— not sin we have overlooked confessing or haven't had a chance yet to confess.

Salvation doesn't depend upon having a perfect memory of sins we commit. Jesus did not ask the thief on the cross to confess his thousands of sins before promising him paradise. The dying man admitted his sinfulness and cast himself upon Christ—and he was saved.

At times all of us, pressured by temptation, momentarily wander from God's will. There's no excuse for this yielding to sin, even though it happens with the best of us. Paul said we all fall short of the glory of God (see Romans 3:23).

Consider Mike and Cindy again. Under stress they may fail each other, saying hasty words that don't reflect the love they really do cherish for each other. Then when the heat cools off, they feel ashamed and deeply sorry. So they confess their sin and make up.

Now tell me. After they have cleared the air with their confession, must they go down to the county courthouse and get married again? Certainly not. However, if they refused to admit their guilt and stubbornly denied their sinfulness, that marriage would ultimately be lost.

Any problem, even something small, can eventually split apart a relationship unless it is confessed and confronted. So in the Christian life. We must confess specific sin—to nip it in the bud before it becomes a cherished sin, something more important to us than Jesus. At that point we would indeed lose our salvation.

Thank God, though, we don't have to live in the dungeon of spiritual insecurity. Having entrusted ourselves to Jesus, we can *know* we are saved, whether or not we *feel* saved.

Feelings often fool us. A friend of our family discovered a tumor. Thank God, her surgeon caught the cancer in time, before it did fatal damage. She had been feeling wonderful, despite the cancer secretly nibbling away at her life. Her feelings deceived her.

Spiritually, too, feelings often fail to tell the truth. We might feel confident about heaven even while lost outside of Christ. And we might feel guilty when everything is fine with our Lord.

In my prayer counseling at the Adventist Media Center, I receive many letters from people like honest-hearted Alice, distressed about lacking peace with God. I tried to comfort her: "You're confusing peaceful *feelings*—which you don't have—with that true peace with God, which you really do have, since you've entrusted your life to Jesus." I went on to explain that peaceful feelings are emotions, which come and go. They do not affect our legal standing of innocence through the blood of Christ.

Newly married couples often don't feel very married, yet they are legally married just the same. So with us spiritually. Whether we *feel* peace, we can *know* that we have forgiveness. "Therefore, having been justified by faith, we have peace with God through our Lord Jesus Christ" (Romans 5:1).

So peaceful feelings are nice, but not necessary to be saved. A surrendered heart entrusted to Christ is what counts.

Give yourself a spiritual checkup. Have you repented of your sins and accepted Jesus as your Saviour and Lord? Then, thank God, your sins are forgiven. When God looks down from heaven, He smiles at you and says, "This is John, my beloved son, in whom I am well pleased."

"Oh, no, Lord," you may protest, "You can't be happy with me. I'm still twenty pounds overweight. After I conquer my appetite, I can consider myself worthy to be Your child."

God responds, "I've got the power for you to overcome your weight problem. But even now you are 'accepted in the Beloved,' 'you are complete in Him' [see Ephesians 1:6; Colossians 2:10]. Not because you are worthy but because you have accepted the life of My Son."

Praise God, He invites us to "rejoice because your names are written in heaven" (Luke 10:20). He wants His true believers to be confident in Christ about salvation. Without such certainty of sins forgiven, wouldn't it be foolish, even irrational, to want probation to close so Jesus can come?

At this point the real objection to assurance surfaces: "If Christians can rest assured of salvation in Christ, they might become lax in their obedience." Indeed, many Adventists do fear that security in Christ will open the floodgates of sin.

At one camp meeting last summer, a lady came up to me beside the platform with concern written across her face: "I'm afraid your message is going to lower our standards and open the floodgates of sin."

I affirmed her concerns about careless Christianity. Then I pointed to the toddlers clinging to her dress and asked, "What keeps you faithful as a mother in feeding your little ones? Is it fear of breaking the child-abuse law that keeps you from becoming a careless parent?"

"No!" she protested, "I feed my children because I love them."

"Well, then," I responded, "if love makes us faithful parents, shouldn't love also be good enough to make us faithful Christians?"

Think about it! How sad that we often relate to our heavenly Father on a lower level than we relate to human beings. Many "Sadventists" remain "faithful" only through guilt and fear. If you cut that leash of legalism, they might run away from religion. But suppose they do? They only expose their own spiritual immaturity. A loyal pet doesn't need a leash to stay by its master's side.

God *wants* us to have the freedom to abandon Him, if we do choose! Ellen White said regarding the Scriptures, "All who look for hooks to hang their doubts upon will find them."[5] If you and I wrote the Bible, we'd make the truth so plain nobody could mistake it. All those troublesome little texts about new moons and sabbath days nailed to the cross and the like—we would remove them all. Yet God in His infinite wisdom has left scores of those little hooks to hang doubts upon. Of course, anybody who really wants to obey the truth can find plenty of evidence. But whoever wants to disobey—and still claim to believe the Bible—has plenty of opportunity to do so.

It's just that way with the assurance of salvation. God leaves opportunity for all who want to abuse gospel freedom to do so—and they may still appear to believe in Jesus. But they are only fooling themselves: "Do not be deceived, God is not mocked; for whatever a man sows, that he will also reap" (Galatians 6:7). We have free choice, but we must bear the consequences.

Even knowing all this, it's still so difficult to let careless people run their course. But does God even want people to obey Him if their motive is legalism? What did Jesus say? *"If you love Me, keep My commandments"* (John 14:15, emphasis supplied).

Confidence in Christ enables us to love God and keep His commandments. Assurance of salvation purifies our dead works of guilt and fear so that we serve the Lord with a heart set free.

One test of gospel freedom is the potential abuse. You can't ferment soda pop—only pure grape juice. And the counterfeit gospel of legalism leaves nothing for carelessness and presumption to ferment—only pure gospel has freedom of forgiveness that can be misused. No wonder the apostle Paul constantly found himself reassuring offended legalists that his gospel of freedom didn't give a green light to lawless living. "God forbid!" he told them.

Think about it. Many shun God's grace because they fear the danger of disgraceful living. But the opposite should be true—if our gospel offers nothing that can be misused or misunderstood, it can't be the true message of the New Testament.

Freedom from guilt opens the floodgates for righteousness. The same paycheck the carouser takes to the tavern Friday night also can provide a faithful breadwinner opportunity to feed the family. So the solution for careless living isn't withholding the paycheck—you can't live without it. Just the same, we must not suppress the free gift of forgiveness.

The gospel can be abused, but we can't really love the Lord without it. "God has not given us a spirit of fear, but of power and of love and of a sound mind" (2 Timothy 1:7).

We *are* children of God—in Christ there is no doubt about it. As surely as we believe the seventh day is the Sabbath, just as certainly we rejoice in being children of God with our sins forgiven.

The Lord doesn't call us to a work bee to finish off our salvation. The gospel invitation is, " 'Come, for all things are now ready' " (Luke 14:17). If we are willing to exchange the world's counterfeit fulfillments for what God offers us in Christ, that act of faith instantly qualifies us for a first-class trip to our celestial home. The Bible says so:

> Giving thanks to the Father who has qualified us to be partakers of the inheritance of the saints in the light. He has delivered us from the power of darkness and translated us into the kingdom of the Son of His love, in whom we have redemption through His blood, the forgiveness of sins (Colossians 1:12-14).

Can you see it? In Christ *right now* we are qualified for that ride through the sky. In fact, the text tells us that God has already translated us, legally speaking. As believers in Jesus, we now sit with Him in heavenly places, citizens of heaven.

It's such a shame when sincere Adventists worry about being worthy of going to heaven—when in Christ they are already up there. All that remains is for Christ to bring us in our new bodies to heaven when He comes again. At this moment we already live there by faith, unworthy though we be. This explains why the burden of the New Testament is not *getting* ready, but *being* ready for Christ's coming. The moment we repent and accept Jesus, we *are* ready to meet Him, instantly qualified as citizens of heaven.

This isn't "once saved, always saved," you understand. We must day by day live by faith in Christ, reaffirming that fundamental exchange of what the world offers for what God offers us.

May the Lord help Seventh-day Adventists everywhere to rejoice in His acceptance. Only then can we love Him with all our hearts as well as our minds and love one another—for this is the law and the prophets.

1. Ellen White, *Christ's Object Lessons*, p. 155.
2. *Ibid.*
3. *Testimonies*, vol. 5, pp. 199, 200.
4. Not their real names.
5. *The Great Controversy*, p. 527.

Chapter 4

Standards That Ring True

(Adornment and Amusements)

Last week while I was across the country in Maine at a camp meeting, my wife back home went roller-skating with another man. Hand in hand they circled the rink as my new rival confided his loneliness for a life partner.

Now, hold the phone. Before you dial 911 and report my wife to your local sheriff, please understand that no one could ask for a more faithful spouse than my Darlene. She's devoted in every way. Though friendly to everyone, she's also conservative in her deportment. Well, why then would she be skating with another man?

You can put the blame on my wife's sincere attempt to uphold Adventist standards. Let me explain what happened. Every Monday night the nearby roller rink caters exclusively to Christians. Believers from various denominations get together and skate to good Christian music, enjoying wholesome fun and fellowship. My wife brought our thirteen-year-old daughter Christie, accompanied by other Pathfinders and their parents.

Everything went well until the magic moment came for couples to skate together. Darlene was heading for the bench when an unfamiliar man rolled up beside her.

"Will you skate with me?"

Before she could say, "No thanks, I'm married," he took her hand, and off they went. Round and round the rink they skated while she tried to let him know she was married without embarrassing him to death. Our friends on the sidelines gleefully witnessed her dilemma. They will never let her forget it. And they had quite a report waiting for me when I arrived home.

Bless their hearts.

Poor Darlene. That fine Christian man assumed she was available because she wasn't wearing a wedding band. Fortunately he wasn't too upset, although I doubt that his introduction to the confusing world of Adventist standards did much to warm his heart toward our church.

After my wife phoned me with the news of her encounter, I thought of another wedding ring episode that happened to Suzy,[1] who is a nurse and the daughter of a conference president. Her experience turned out to be less than funny.

For several weeks a respected young physician had been saying Hi to Suzy when he passed the nurses' station on his way to the operating room. She thought nothing of it. Everybody was friendly like that.

Then one morning he remarked, "You know, that smile of yours really brightens my day."

That got Suzy worried.

The next morning while passing by, the doctor paused and waited for her to look up. Almost timidly he posed the question: "Would you join me for dinner after work today?"

Suzy blushed and stammered, "I can't. You see, I'm married."

"Married!" Disappointment and dismay flooded the doctor's face. He felt betrayed. For a few seconds he just stood there, as if watching his love boat sink. Then his eyes narrowed. "You're deceitful! If you're married, you ought to be wearing a wedding ring." With that, he picked up his charts and strode away.

Nothing Suzy could say from that day onward could relieve the doctor's resentment. Her faithfulness to church standards brought embarrassment to a well-meaning man and ruined their professional relationship.

Such wedding ring stories are familiar to Adventists across North America. Are these uncomfortable and unprofitable encounters really necessary? Ponder that thought in the light of this story.

A young Russian czar, many years ago, enjoyed taking walks in the royal garden. One day he noticed a palace guard nearby, standing in all his pomp and ceremony, watching over what appeared to be nothing.

Curious, the czar came over and asked the young soldier what he was guarding. He didn't know—except that orders called for a sentry at that spot.

The young czar searched the records. He discovered that at one time, Catherine the Great had sponsored acres of rare rose gardens. On that spot a choice and beautiful rosebush had grown. Every week the queen permitted the peasants to come and view the roses, but she ordered a sentry to stand guard over that particular bush. The order was never rescinded. The rose gardens had long since disappeared, yet a sentry still stood guard—over nothing at all.

Could it be that in our time we, too, may find ourselves sincerely standing guard over things not sacred at all? We Adventists warn our Sunday-keeping friends about the futility of human tradition. But I wonder whether we, too, have a lesson to learn. In maintaining some of our cherished standards, are we merely standing guard over nothing but outdated tradition?

"Tradition!" someone protests. "It's the wedding ring that's based upon pagan tradition."

Well, have you ever stopped to think just how many innocent customs in our culture come to us from paganism? Consider the days of the week, named after pagan planet worship. Sunday to worship the sun, Monday to worship the moon, and on through the week.

Roger Coon of the Ellen G. White Estate notes that "in the earlier days of Adventism our pioneers refused to use the common names of the days of the week [Sunday, Monday, Tuesday, and so on], choosing instead to speak of 'First day,' 'Second day,' 'Third day,' etc. They felt that the commonly used names possessed pagan connotations that devout Christians should eschew. A bit later our leaders abandoned this distinction in favor of returning to the more conventional names used by everyone else. Why? Because the alleged pagan connection was simply no longer significant in contemporary culture." [2]

Coon then nails down his point: "Would it be illogical to conclude, therefore, that a custom's origin in the paganism of antiquity does not provide sufficient reason for abandoning it?"[3]

Do you get it? Just because we say it's Monday today doesn't mean we worship the moon. And just because the Dorcas leader wears a wedding ring doesn't mean she's a pagan prostitute.

Lots of innocent customs in our Anglo-Saxon culture come to us from paganism. Here's a real stunner. You know how the minister shakes your hand after the sermon when you exit the church. Can you guess where that time-honored tradition descended from?

Brace yourself as you read the fascinating book published by Harper and Row, *Extraordinary Origins of Everyday Things*:[4] "In its oldest recorded use [2800 B.C., Egypt], a handshake signified the conferring of power from a god to an earthly ruler." Pagan priests then passed on that power to the people when, following a service honoring the sun god, they shook the hands of the worshipers to symbolically endow them with divine power. This book further documents that ancient Babylon and Assyria also used the ceremonial handshake in their pagan worship.

How about that!

One of our popular evangelists zealously condemns the worldly standards he sees infiltrating the Adventist Church. He's a friend of mine, so I don't mind teasing him a bit. I pointed out that by his own standard of shunning everything of pagan origin, he must now quit shaking hands after his sermons. A high-five slap might be more appropriate. (Perhaps even the holy kiss of the New Testament.)

Nothing doing. I saw him later that day shaking somebody's hand after the finest tradition of pagan sun worship.

The next time I saw him, I had a little more fun with him. "Let me ask your advice about jewelry," I began innocently. "I notice you're wearing a bracelet."

"That's not a bracelet—that's my watch!" he protested.

"Well, take a look at this new watch I just got." And I pulled from my pocket a silver ring that had a tiny watch inside it, complete with a second hand ticking.

"This ring, just like your bracelet, serves a useful purpose by telling time. Do you see any moral difference between your bracelet and my ring?"

"Let me see that thing," he growled. After staring at it a moment, he frowned. "No, it's not OK to wear that ring. It looks too much like adornment."

"On the contrary." I smiled. "This ring watch is actually much smaller and less flashy than your bracelet watch. Besides, in addition to telling the time, it serves the added purpose of showing that I'm married to my wife instead of living in sin."

My friend shifted his feet uneasily as I pressed the point.

"Don't you see, this ring demonstrates to the world that I honor the seventh commandment. You believe in keeping the commandments, don't you?"

"Of course! But wearing that ring isn't going to keep you faithful to your wife. People commit adultery all the time wearing a wedding ring."

"Yes, but at least it helps close the door to temptation. Decent people in society respect the sign of a wedding ring. Common courtesy demands that, you know," I reminded him.

My friend wasn't going to surrender his war against the wedding ring, even though he was fighting without ammunition. He changed gears and tried a new approach:

"Not wearing a ring provides our members wonderful opportunities to witness about the message. When someone asks a married woman for a date, she can share her faith about our standards."

"Well," I responded, "first of all, I'm not sure that people we embarrass and disappoint are prepared to appreciate our message. And just because you try to explain your opposition to the wedding ring doesn't mean you will convince anyone. Intelligent people are not going to be fooled by our inconsistencies in upholding the standards."

At this point my good-natured friend was getting weary of our discussion. He concluded, "All I can say is that God's Holy Word forbids the wearing of adornment."

"But how can you call this ring an adornment when it tells me the time and also shows that I'm a commandment keeper?"

So the conversation went. There was no way my good friend was going to let the truth get in the way of his tradition.

Please don't get me wrong. I appreciate this evangelist's sincerity and his interest in maintaining Christian standards. All I ask is that we be logical and consistent in upholding them—and that we have a little mercy in our minds for those who may not see everything just as we do.

By the way, don't lose any sleep over my little ring—I use it only for illustration purposes. Wearing that silly thing wouldn't be worth the world war that would break out if one of your local extremists spotted it!

Seventh-day Adventist doctrines are so perfectly logical that Satan cannot refute them. So he inspires zealous saints to invent conditions of church membership that are illogical and indefensible. Devilishly clever, wouldn't you say?

They aren't the only ones who suffer loss. Thousands of committed Christians, responding to our doctrines, find themselves barred from entering our church because they cannot make sense out of our standards. And it isn't just our neighbors who are turned away—tragically, we are losing our own precious children by the droves. How can we demand their commitment to standards we ourselves can't explain?

We blame worldliness for the prevailing laxity in our church. But is our current avalanche of liberalization also due, at least in part, to the inadequate and outmoded arguments employed in upholding our standards?

Something to think about.

Along with losing our children over inconsistent standards, many Adventist wives have seen the souls of their husbands lost. Read this letter I received recently:

> On May 23 I am being baptized into the Adventist Church. My husband opposes my decision because of the jewelry issue. He doesn't understand why I had to remove the wedding band. And so this has been a difficult step which I have prayed about constantly. I pray that my husband's heart will soften and he will see the beauty of our message so he will also be baptized.

Maybe someday this man will join the Adventist Church. Chances are he will not. Take a look around your local church. Why are all those married women sitting alone? In thousands of cases, the husband's alienation toward our faith began the day the wedding ring came off. These men perceived that our church was interfering with their marriage. All they know is that a strange man made their wives remove the symbol of faithfulness to their wedding vows.

Thank God, despite vigorous opposition from some members, the Adventist Church permits candidates for baptism to honor their own conscience when it comes to wedding bands. Pastors have no right to require them to remove a simple wedding ring, any more than they can force them to stop watching television or become vegetarians. Despite their good intentions, pastors who insist upon setting up their own standards as the gateway to church membership are operating in violation of official church policy.

At the same time General Conference leaders voted to allow wedding bands, they reaffirmed our church's historic stand against adornment. The big question, of course, is, What constitutes adornment?

At the airport recently I met a Mennonite man in a plain black suit who doesn't believe in wearing neckties. He thinks they are a useless adornment, nothing but a cloth necklace. I wasn't sure what to tell him. After all, what utilitarian purpose does a tie serve—except to keep my neck warm on a hot summer day? Obviously, standards of adornment vary according to one's own culture and conscience.

How about wearing makeup? Should it be condemned as illegal adornment, even if its purpose is to appear natural? Here at the Adventist Media Center, all guests of the various telecasts must wear makeup on camera. For the sake of self-gratification? Not at all. Yet some would condemn this as a violation of historic standards. Can you and I disagree on standards and both of us remain Adventists in good standing?

Of course, certain beliefs are beyond disagreement. Immorality stands condemned, along with gossip, lethargy, racism, and so forth. Beyond these basic requirements of Christian behavior we Seventh-day Adventists have pillars of faith that distinguish us, such as the Sabbath, the second coming, and the sanctuary. Within the circle of these nonnegotiable truths there is room for individual interpretation. Regarding such matters, the apostle Paul said, "Let each be fully persuaded in his own mind" (Romans 14:5). "So then each of us shall give account of himself to God" (verse 12).

Notice Paul didn't say we can just do as we please. We obey the voice of God as it persuades us in our own mind, our conscience.

Some people have problems with such liberty. One lady told me, "We must present a united front to the world. When visitors to our church find some people wearing wedding bands and others not, they become confused. How can we explain such divergence in behavior?"

Well, how do we explain the fact that some of our people own televisions and some don't? The answer is simple. God has created each of us with an individual conscience. Remember, the Adventist Church is not a cult. Members need some elbow room.

Not long ago the following letter arrived in my office. "All week long I've hardly been able to sleep well because some of our members are wearing wedding bands. They are splitting the church apart."

Imagine the power of a little wedding ring to split an entire church! Who is to blame for such a tragedy? Members who quietly wear their symbol of holy wedlock—or those who won't leave them alone?

Think about it. Whom does God hold accountable for conflict in the congregation—the wealthy couple wearing diamond-studded Rolex watches or the new convert they condemned for wearing a wedding ring? Do you blame the deaconess with a gaudy brooch the size of a silver dollar—or the lady she denounced for wearing a tiny Christian cross suspended from a thin, nearly unnoticeable necklace?

I don't think wearing cross necklaces is worth waging war over, even for the notice of bearing testimony for Christ. So I always counsel new members to remove them lest there be a tempest in the teapot. Actually, though, shouldn't the burden of maintaining the peace be borne by older members trying to believe the best about babes in Christ? Can't they be kind and tolerant instead of chasing them out of the church?

At one Midwestern camp meeting, a pastor's wife was conducting a seminar on how to dress and act like an attractive Christian. Her goal was to help the ladies feel good about themselves, look good for their husbands, and present a good witness to the community. Her material was sensible and presented in fine taste, but a swarm of hornets attacked her as a compromiser. You would have thought she was teaching a class on how to brew a batch of moonshine!

I'm wondering if the accusers of that poor pastor's wife might have been happier spending camp-meeting week in a medieval convent. Nobody there worries about looking attractive. Maybe they should have made a pilgrimage to fundamentalist Iran under Ayatollah Khomeini, whose eternal frown enforced Allah's militant dress reform. Perhaps they would have been happy in Communist China during the reign of Chairman Mao, who purged everything pretty and pleasant.

One thing seems certain—those angry saints didn't have the spirit of Christ anymore than Khomeini or Mao Tse-tung did. All showed the same source of inspiration. And I'm afraid that all will share the same eternity. How very sad. We will deal further with the problem of criticism and gossip in a later chapter.

Before we set ourselves up as worthy models of upholding Adventist standards, remember this. Lots of things in our lives can betray needless luxury, including the kind of car we drive. Some care only about adornment hung on the body. Adornment on one's clothes or adornment on wheels is OK. Explain that for me, would you?

Or better yet, try to explain it to your kids. And while you are at it, tell them why they shouldn't go to movies.

I think we have a strong case against theater attendance. Not that demons lurk in the dark corners of the building itself. Rather, I think that demons infest the minds of most Hollywood scriptwriters. Pitifully few movies might be worth watching anywhere—at the theater, in the school auditorium, or at home.

It's strange that some members who faithfully avoid the theater feel it's perfectly OK to watch those same movies in the living room. Does an Adventist VCR player somehow sanctify an R-rated movie?

I think Christians should generally avoid theaters for several reasons. For one thing, the expense involved. Movies aren't so cheap anymore, from what I hear. Beyond that, we need to remember that revenue from tickets supports Hollywood's stars and studios in their sin business. There's also the influence factor. If I go to Walt Disney's *Bambi* this week, someone who trusts my example might see a bad movie next week.

My reasoning here is debatable. Some would say it costs no more to see a movie than it does to go to Dodger Stadium. Besides, attendance at the occasional good movie from Hollywood shows the studios that clean fun can be profitable, thus encouraging them to clean up their act. As for one's influence, perhaps people ought to have enough sense to know that I'm going to see *Bambi* instead of *Rambo*.

I could counter with other arguments, such as the time wasted in questionable wreck-reation. Also the fact that it's easier to switch channels at home when necessary than to walk out of a dark and crowded theater. This discussion has no cut-and-dried solution, I admit.

For the first time in twenty years, I recently entered a theater to see a new Billy Graham film with my children. I wanted them to get a spiritual blessing unavailable elsewhere, and they certainly did. But do you know, some Adventists would have condemned me for seeing that Christian movie in a theater—while they themselves at home were watching some marginally risqué television program?

Really, though, the most serious problem with programming of any kind is not so much the evil as the secular. We tend to take pride in our squeaky-clean telecast preferences, forgetting that the basic temptation of sin is simply to live outside of Christ. Hollywood's biggest lie is that we can find fulfillment in a clean and caring lifestyle without fellowship with God. Wholesome worldliness, more than the heat of porno passion, divorces lukewarm members from their Lord. Sportscasts can outscore the Saviour in the competition for our commitment. And even innocent family shows, in modeling morality without reference to God, probably do more than anything else to secularize our lives and ruin our dependence upon grace.

Hard to believe? Take inventory: Do Bill Cosby and the Huxtables have family worship? Do they encourage one another with Bible promises? People can be cute, popular, smart, successful, and even loving while ignoring God in daily life. The influence of this godless, artificial morality may affect us more than we realize.

When was the last time you enjoyed a non-Sabbath evening reading God's Word? Do you visit the poor and the sick? No time? Why are we so tied up? Maybe we would find freedom to live for God if we diminished our dependence upon television. Rather than staying up late watching the bad news, we could be getting up early for the Good News. Perhaps we have a Christian experience that is "*for* the birds" because we do not rise *with* the birds to praise God for the dawning day and welcome His fellowship.

What it boils down to is this: If we don't have time to read the Bible and the inspired writings of Ellen White as we should, how do we defend our extensive involvement in secular entertainment?

All in all, we might do well to avoid theaters under normal circumstances. As for the TV at home, if we can't control it, let's get rid of it—without criticizing those among us who do manage quite well in controlling the tube.

Now, on a lighter note, shall we talk about diet?

---

1. Not her real name.

2. Roger Coon, "Reviving Ancient Paganism," *Adventist Review*, June 11, 1987, p. 9.

3. *Ibid*.

4. All this is documented in Charles Panati, *Extraordinary Originals of Everyday Things* (New York: Harper and Row, 1987), pp. 42, 43.

Chapter 5

The Pantry Patrol

(Diet and Dress Reform)

Gravel crunches in your driveway as a large black-and-white van rolls up. Oh, no! It's the Pantry Patrol conducting their weekly food inspection.

Seven commandos jump out of the van, their stiffly starched uniforms flapping in the breeze. Marching as to war, they approach your front door. Get out of the way or get stampeded!

They shove themselves inside and charge toward your kitchen, handcuffs clinking at their sides. At this moment they are peering inside your fridge.

Let's see . . . Good! You are finally eating tofu hot dogs. And your pickles are now bathing in lemon juice rather than vinegar. But what's this here? You still have a drinking problem, with milk from a cow! Don't you know that the Patrol control board voted that the time has come for you to dispense with dairy products?

A dark mark now smudges your status chart. All things considered, though, you are doing better. Making progress.

The Patrol commandos silently nod their blessing as they troop out the door.

Whew! You survived another investigative judgment (as if the one going on in heaven were not enough). Good thing the Patrol didn't spot the cheesecake you hid in the freezer behind the organic Swiss chard.

The next day's mail brings an official notice from the captain of the Pantry Patrol. You are tentatively approved to serve for another month as Sabbath School song leader. Knees buckling in relief, you sink into the nearest chair. And then you find yourself wondering. Shouldn't there be room in the church for those who may not be ready to consign Elsie the cow to the ranks of the unemployed?

Of course I've exaggerated with my little parody, but we all know that food has always been a real hot potato for Seventh-day Adventists. I'm not just trying to be funny—both freedom of conscience and spiritual responsibility are at stake in this battle between health reform and health deform. Each of us must personally face the challenge of God's Word: "Do you not know that your body is the temple of the Holy Spirit who is in you, whom you have from God, and you are not your own? For you were bought at a price; therefore glorify God in your body and in your spirit, which are God's" (1 Corinthians 6:19, 20).

No doubt about it. It certainly does matter how we treat the temple God gave us to live in. We have a solemn obligation to glorify the Saviour in what we put in and put on our bodies. But honestly, I don't know if the time has come for me to stop indulging in frozen yogurt. I hope not. I do know the time has come to stop indulging in criticism.

You might be wondering if I'm saying all this to defend secret compromises in my own life. Relax. Like most Adventist ministers, I'm not wearing earrings or makeup today. One potential item of controversy is the way I fasten my tie so it won't dip into my soybean soup. I used to use a safety pin, humbly hidden out of sight, but nowadays I venture out of the house sporting a tiny round tie tack.

Is that OK?

As for my eating habits, it's been more than twenty years since I've had lunch under the golden arches with Ronald McDonald. (That was about seventy billion burgers ago.) You might also be delighted to know that I haven't eaten eggs for about eighteen years, three months, and twelve days. (Can anybody on the Pantry Patrol match that awesome attainment?) Nevertheless, I don't mind if my kids fry themselves an omelet. The Christian life for teens is straight and narrow enough without additional strictures from me.

Now, let's forget about food for a while and think about holiday observance. Does freedom of conscience apply to Christmas and Easter celebration (there's that word again!)? Why not? Despite the suffocating secularism in society, these holidays can remind us of Jesus. Many thoughtful parents capitalize on the spirit of the season by highlighting the Christian aspects of Christmas and Easter. Those holidays don't involve breaking any commandment of God, as does Sunday in violation of the fourth commandment.

Again we see the need for personal freedom of interpretation regarding standards of conduct. Rules regulating behavior are not all written on tables of stone. For example, in New Testament days, modesty required women to cover their heads in church (see 1 Corinthians 11:5). Such is no longer the case. And over the last century, standards of modesty have continued to change. Despite that, some Adventists seem determined to make every woman look like a prairie pioneer of the 1870s. Or maybe a Russian babushka.

You know, mega-length dresses. Collars that tickle the chin. Grandma Moses hairdos. No makeup. Nothing pretty or attractive.

Is this what God requires of us? Or is this the devil's way of turning off fellow Christians who might otherwise be attracted to our wonderfully sensible doctrines?

We must know the difference between principles and standards. Principles are unchanging, fundamental values. Standards are rules for behavior that apply principles—rules that must change to keep pace with society. Ironically, sometimes, maintaining our values actually requires transgressing previous rules.

Back in 1968, when I got my driver's license, the state of New Jersey taught me it was a sin to make a right turn on a red light. Now it's legal. Should I condemn the legislators for lowering the standards of obedience to traffic laws? Or should I simply accept the fact that no moral issues are involved, and drivers are actually better off now?

Suppose I stubbornly cling to the past and refuse to turn

right on red. Am I anymore righteous than other drivers—or am I simply causing traffic jams?

You see the point. Sincere but misguided members cause problems in the church by refusing to update their standards.

The fact is that our church must adjust its standards of behavior to keep pace with reality, while basic Christian principles remain unchanged. Why is this so hard for some of us to understand?

We don't want to get soft on sin, of course. Every faithful Adventist feels deeply about creeping compromise, worldliness in the church. This is a serious matter for each conscience to address individually and prayerfully.

Strict obedience to God's standards as I understand them is not necessarily legalism. Motivation is the key. If my goal is to become good enough to deserve a trip to heaven, that's legalism. Dead works. But if my goal is to honor my Lord in gratitude for His salvation—seeking to bring every deed and thought into harmony with His will—that's love.

A devoted wife is fussy about fixing her husband's food just the way he wants it, and when he wants it. That's not legalism. It's love.

Love is particular. Love wants to get it right. But love cannot be legislated by church councils.

Many Adventists would be delighted if the Ellen G. White Estate handed down a detailed list of do's and don'ts for every imaginable situation in life. Then they could escape the responsibility of discerning God's will for themselves, blindly following human leaders. Such a list would also strengthen their hand in policing fellow church members.

But no thanks. Let's leave some room for individual conscience. People willing to make the big commitment for baptism and church membership can surely be trusted with little decisions involving diet, dress, and entertainment. At least God seems to think so.

Regarding the essentials of the faith, we must have unity. In nonessentials, tolerance. In all things, charity. That's the Christian way.

Chapter 6

Sister Stern

(Counterfeit Holiness)

Sister Stern would have been a good name for her. Just the look on her hard, gray face made me shiver. Her piercing eyes could have struck terror in the heart of Ivan the Terrible.

Sister Stern trod the straight-and-narrow tightrope all her life. No worldly television. No happy music of any kind. No amusements, questionable or otherwise. Her idea of a big evening was to go to bed early with one of her red books and turn the electric blanket up to medium.

She lived by those books as zealously as anyone I've known. The one most underlined was *Counsels on Diet and Foods*. It was her guidebook for living, her blueprint for a transformed character worthy of heaven.

No milk. No cheese. No eggs. Sugar—are you kidding?

Despite her no-fat, high-fiber diet, Sister Stern suffered from constipation—her conscience was so constipated by legalism that she never knew freedom in Jesus. Health reform became her gospel. She scoffed at the shallow spirituality of church members who got sick. If only they lived up to the standards she upheld, none of these diseases would come upon them.

Then the impossible happened to Sister Stern. She was struck with cancer. The doctor said she didn't have much time left.

But no, she knew better. God was only letting the devil test

her. He would never allow someone so faithful as she to die in spiritual shame. Surely He was obliged to restore her as a testimony to her lofty faith.

As Sister Stern's pastor, I tried to prepare her for whatever God's will might be, life or death. My greatest concern was that she finally put her trust in Christ's mercy rather than the counterfeit merit of personal perfection. That way she could go to heaven and have peace on earth in her final hours.

But no. When I visited her, Sister Stern rejected my concept of "cheap grace." In fact, she practically ordered me to leave her trailer, accusing my gospel of opening the floodgates of sin. And so, I'm afraid, the floodgates of mercy remained closed to her soul.

Reluctant to abandon her to perish in such misery, I asked one of my associates to visit her. "Just hold her hand and read her the Psalms," I suggested. So he did, day after day.

Sister Stern's adult daughters stayed by her side as well, despite the fact that her perfectionistic parenting spoiled their memories of childhood. Mother had always demanded that even their words be strictly sacred in character—harmless teenage slang sparked a scathing rebuke. All this suffocated her relationship with the ones God gave her to love and lead. Nevertheless they faithfully supported her as the end drew near.

As time dragged on, Sister Stern finally realized that God was not going to heal her. Her "firm foundation" turned out to be quicksand. Sinking fast, she felt betrayed by everything she stood for. Tremendous resentment began to surface.

One afternoon it erupted in a shocking outburst. With the pastor sitting nearby, the home nurse asked Sister Stern, "Would you like a little whole-wheat toast with your favorite sesame butter?"

"No!" she roared, clenching a fist. "The h--l with that! Fry me an egg!"

Sister Stern eating an egg? That was like an orthodox rabbi eating a pork chop. It was her ultimate expression of bitterness against the God who refused to recognize her righteousness. She was shaking her fist at the spiritual lifestyle that left her devastated in both body and soul.

How tragic! All through the years Sister Stern had seemed like such a strong Adventist, glorying in the power of God to perfect the life and purify the body. Pity the compromiser who crossed her path. But the hour of death exposed her own pitiful, weak faith.

The Bible helps us understand holy weaklings like Sister Stern. These people consider themselves strong specimens of spirituality because they support strong standards—yet they are weak in faith. Their hope is based on something less than Jesus' blood and righteousness. They major in minors.

"One believes he may eat all things, but he who is weak eats only vegetables" (Romans 14:2).

He who is weak eats only vegetables? What could that mean? Let's get the background.

The discussion in Romans is not about vegetarianism itself or clean versus unclean meat. The bone of contention involved meat offered to idols, a matter of major controversy in the first-century church. We see this in 1 Corinthians 8:4:

"Concerning the eating of things offered to idols, we know that an idol is nothing in the world, and that there is no other God but one."

In other words, since Paul recognized only one God, his conscience didn't care whether the meat he ate had been offered to idols. So he concluded: "Food does not commend us to God; for neither if we eat are we the better, nor if we do not eat are we the worse" (verse 8).

Yet he also realized that "there is not in everyone that knowledge" (verse 7). These weaker Christians, in their sincere ignorance, worried so much about offending God by eating meat offered to idols that they restricted their diet to vegetables. "Their conscience, being weak, is defiled" (verse 7).

A weak conscience, weak in faith. Defiled by fear and guilt. Majoring in minors while minoring in that which is truly important.

We have here a vital new dimension in our concept of spiritual weakness. Usually we consider a weak believer to be a compromiser, someone whose laid-back conscience is lounging on the Riviera. But there is also an opposite kind of weakness

when the conscience becomes an unsmiling tyrant, forever shaking its bony finger in our faces. This hyperactive holiness forbids assurance in Christ and produces discouragement. Faith is crippled.

Many Christians with that kind of weak conscience seem strong at first because they come on so strong against sin. They don't realize that their scrupulous sensitivities deceive them, pretending to speak for God.

Think about it. Are we automatically on God's side when we condemn something sinful?

Remember the Ayatollah Khomeini, who waged war against worldliness in Iran? He condemned America as the Great Satan for its beer and bikinis—but he ridiculed the Christian faith. Obviously he wasn't a spiritual powerhouse simply because he condemned sin. He wasn't even a Christian!

How would you define Christianity? "That's simple," someone suggests. "Christianity is just being like Jesus, living the way He did."

No, that's not Christianity. That's more like Hinduism.

The Indian leader Gandhi was so charmed by the example of Jesus that he walked the dusty roads of India and lived as Jesus did, a nonviolent life of love. *He accepted Christ as his example but not as his substitute.* Gandhi specifically rejected the blood atonement of Jesus Christ. In place of Christian faith he taught that salvation was a gradual process of character perfection, the purging of bad "karma."

Weak Christians are not quite like Gandhi—they do believe in Christ's sacrifice for sin; but their faith is fragile. They trust Christ's blood to cover their past sins, but not to qualify them for heaven. Their goal for eternal life is attaining a perfect character, the same hope Gandhi had.

Can you see why these perfectionists are weak in faith despite their sincere warfare against sin? Remember, just because I condemn evil does not prove I'm a well-rounded Christian. You may recall the public clash between rock star Ozzie Osbourne and Cardinal John O'Connor. Osbourne, of satanic Black Sabbath fame, locked horns with O'Connor after the New York archbishop condemned the demonic images in his music. Obviously Ozzie

Osbourne doesn't represent God. But does that automatically put heaven's seal of approval on the spiritual leadership of the Roman Catholic cardinal?

Remember those two ditches we've been talking about—permissiveness and legalism. Ozzie Osbourne personifies permissiveness. Catholic teaching suffers from legalism. Both traps are from the devil. And you can backslide either way.

Have you thought about it? People who pull out of permissiveness often drift across the gospel freeway into legalism. The prodigal indulging in worldliness wasn't the only backslider in the family. His brother toiling in the fields of legalism had backslidden as well, estranged from the Father's grace.

Throughout the history of God's people, you see problems both with permissiveness and with legalism. The early Israelites backslid into worldliness when they danced around the golden calf. Deeper and deeper they descended into sin until they finally had to be carried off to Babylon. There, in captivity, they learned their bitter lesson. But they slipped into the opposite ditch. By the time Christ came, they were so entrapped in legalism that they murdered their Messiah in the name of Moses.

Actually, their spiritual condition was worse than in the days of their worldliness. Jesus declared that even the harlots were closer to the kingdom than the righteous terrorists of His day.

The Christian church followed in the footsteps of Jewish apostasy. The Laodiceans plunged into permissiveness, while in other places, such as Ephesus, believers lapsed into legalism. Jesus told the church there: "I know your works, your labor, your patience, and that you cannot bear those who are evil. And that you have tested those who say they are apostles and are not, and have found them liars" (Revelation 2:2).

No problem with laxity in Ephesus—they were on fire for the law. If people of the "new theology" showed up in church, those legalistic zealots chased them out of town. But all that zeal for the law masked a major problem:

"Nevertheless I have this against you, that you have left your first love. Remember therefore from where you have fallen; repent and do the first works" (verses 4, 5).

Repent of what—worldliness? No, repent of legalism. They

had fallen from their first love for Christ into a weak Christianity deficient in faith. They needed the joy of salvation as their strength. They could serve the Lord out of appreciation rather than appeasement.

As time went on, the Christian church of the early centuries slid deeper into legalism. Monastic communities sprouted in the desert for the purpose of perfecting characters in order to escape purgatory. In the year 249 the church father Origen taught that believers didn't qualify as saints until their characters approached perfection. Bishops everywhere echoed such legalism. This church, so polluted by righteousness, became the antichrist power of the Dark Ages. Martin Luther reintroduced the grace of God into that medieval midnight. Rome refused his Reformation, and has retained that basic legalism to this day.

It's hard to believe, but true. You can get up at five every morning to pray and still be a weak Christian—if you don't trust the blood of Christ for your acceptance with God. Legalists who agonize to be worthy are just as weak in faith as Christians who have no devotional life.

You may have heard about Trappist monks who arise for prayer every morning at two o'clock. Does that remarkable display of spiritual discipline necessarily qualify them as strong Christians? Buddhist monks also have early-morning devotions, as do Muslim mullahs. Evidently you can have a strong commitment to spirituality while rejecting faith in Christ. Long ago the Pharisees proved that by fasting twice a week and praying a lot while plotting to crucify Jesus. The helpless harlots had more hope of heaven than those respected spiritual zealots, Christ said.

Would you permit me a word of personal testimony? I used to fast from food and try to pray all night, yet I was miserably weak in faith. My pursuit of perfection compelled me to quit my studies at Columbia Union College and join an independent Adventist commune, where I met some like-minded holy weaklings. As time went on, some of my fellow legalists wearied of their works to the point of abandoning religion entirely. They left the institution and plunged into permissive-

ness. Others there who managed to stay with the "straight testimony," I'm afraid, secretly abandoned their sincerity and succumbed to hypocrisy. Only God knows the heart, but pretended holiness would disqualify us from Christianity altogether and doom us with the Pharisees of Christ's day.

Believers who are weak in faith have not yet abandoned themselves to such hypocrisy. They do sincerely trust in Jesus, or they wouldn't be Christians at all. But they waver in the balance between law and grace, just as careless weaklings on the other extreme waver between sin and surrender. Only God knows when the line is crossed and weak believers forfeit faith altogether—the permissive ones abandoning themselves to sin, and the scrupulous ones abandoning themselves to legalism.

The church of Galatia had crossed the line into damnation, having turned away from "the grace of Christ, to a different gospel" (Galatians 1:6). By abandoning themselves to legalism, they had squandered their salvation: "You have become estranged from Christ, you who attempt to be justified by law; you have fallen from grace" (Galatians 5:4).

So the Galatians had actually ceased to be Christians! Was that the state of Sister Stern? I'm afraid it was. But God alone knows if she had sold her soul to legalism unto her own damnation, or if she was a holy weakling hanging on by a thread to faith in Christ.

It's tragic, but true. Many "good, solid Adventists" will be lost, like the former Christians in Galatia. They may seem so sincere, but when in their blind zeal they reject God's grace, they also reject the only hope of salvation.

Last year I went to a camp meeting where a popular speaker packed the big tent for the Sabbath sermon. He preached a fiery message about Christians needing to attain sinless characters so they can make it to heaven. He condemned the compromising attitudes he saw infiltrating into the church, but he failed to bring repentant sinners the rest and assurance from Calvary. Everybody in the audience seemed totally intimidated and guilt stricken. Everybody, that is, but the Sister Stern–type members. They spent the after-

noon singing the praises of what they supposed was a "good old Adventist sermon."

Without the assurance of God's acceptance, any obedience inspired by that sermon was based on guilt and fear—dead works.

We have clear and compelling counsel about preaching sermons that center in the cross: "The sacrifice of Christ as an atonement for sin is the great truth around which all other truths cluster . . . the Son of God uplifted on the cross. This is to be the foundation of every discourse given by our ministers."[1]

So proclaiming the cross is not something optional. Sermons on standards devoid of the blood of Christ belong in a fundamentalist Muslin mosque or in an Orthodox Jewish synagogue. Not in a Christian church.

How can genuinely committed Christians be so prone to forget the gospel? We want to play it safe in this evil world. We want to overcome all sin and be like Jesus. The enemy of our souls, sensing our sincerity, tempts us to compete with Christ's righteousness rather than accept our Lord's accomplishments as our own. He diverts our attention from the cross to focus upon our own attainments in spiritual growth.

Can you see the danger here? An attitude of faithfulness does not make us immune to a faithless gospel. The devil takes fiendish delight in hijacking a tender conscience and steering it into legalism.

Here's how it happens. Sincere Christians often find themselves afraid of gospel freedom—afraid of what they might do with it. So they barricade themselves from the world with a wall of guilt and fear to safeguard against sin. In doing this they also shut themselves away from the sunlight of assurance in Christ.

Suppose that, back in the Garden of Eden, one of the angels had suggested a fence around the tree of temptation to prevent the spread of sin. God would have responded, "No! I believe in freedom despite the risk of sin. So let's give Adam and Eve their freedom, then see what they do with it. That will be their test."

The Sister Sterns of today are so afraid of abusing gospel freedom that they put a barbed-wire fence around the cross.

They think they are doing the Lord a favor by preventing sinful indulgence. Unfortunately, what they are really doing is denying that "where the Spirit of the Lord is, there is liberty" (2 Corinthians 3:17).

Some husbands and wives make the same mistake in their marriages. They try to keep their spouses faithful through dire threats of what would happen should they stray. Such threats are intended to protect the marriage, but instead they cut out the heart of the relationship. Wise spouses secure the marriage by fostering an atmosphere of acceptance.

Love is the only true safeguard. That's why Jesus said, *"If you love Me*, keep My commandments" (John 14:15, emphasis supplied). Obedience of love fueled by appreciation for forgiveness is the only type of obedience God wants. Anything else amounts to dead works.

Never forget it—people who need that barbed-wire fence of legalism to keep them faithful to God are weak Christians. They may seem so strong, but regarding faith in Christ they are so weak. So all those right-wing publications that major in guilt and fear are the product of weak Christians—well-meaning though they may be.

I'm afraid that those "ministries" may try to uphold the standards of obedience, but they are entrapped by the fatal legalism of the religious zealots in Christ's day. Jesus warned, "Woe to you, scribes and Pharisees, hypocrites! For you pay tithe of mint and anise and cumin, and have neglected the weightier matters of the law: justice and mercy and faith" (Matthew 23:23). Sister Stern–style Adventists waste hours arguing over nonessential technicalities. If you let them have their way, they would turn church business meetings into inquisitions for persecuting people who wear wedding rings.

How ironic. Holy weaklings shun outward adornment of any kind, yet their inner lives are unadorned by a likeness to Christ. In some cases you don't have to analyze their theology to reject their gospel. Just the look on their faces betrays their weakness. They lack the fruit of the Spirit: "Love, joy, peace, longsuffering, kindness" (Galatians 5:22).

Without love, holy weaklings fail the acid test of Christian-

ity. Jesus said, "By this all will know that you are My disciples, if you have love for one another" (John 13:35). A legalist even fails the test of the law he loves to talk about, for "love is the fulfillment of the law" (Romans 13:10).

How can this be? Jesus said, "To whom little is forgiven, the same loves little" (Luke 7:47). A proud legalist doesn't think he needs forgiveness much. Therefore he doesn't love much. That means he doesn't keep the law much. Amazing, isn't it?

The flower children of the sixties talked about love all the time yet didn't know what it was about. Likewise, holy weaklings talk about the law all the time but don't know what it's about. In their pursuit of holiness, they neglect to "put on love, which is the bond of perfection" (Colossians 3:14).

Holy weaklings lack joy, because they have no assurance of salvation to relieve the Sadventism. They lack peace, since they live in dread of the judgment. They lack longsuffering and kindness, despite the words of their favorite author, which point out that "man's inhumanity to man is his greatest sin." (In other words, it's even worse to criticize and gossip than it is to munch on a Big Mac). Their hearts are just too hard to be touched by homelessness and racism.

Legalists don't care much about the poor. They revere the Sabbath, but they shun its spirit of resting in Christ, revealed in works of mercy. They glory in their health reform and fasting, ignorant that God said, "Is this not the fast that I have chosen: to . . . let the oppressed go free . . . . Is it not to share your bread with the hungry, and that you bring to your house the poor who are cast out?" (Isaiah 58:6, 7).

Do you see the problem? Holy weaklings promote the power of the Spirit but lack His fruit in their lives.

Now here's the big shocker. Legalists are often weak on victory over sin. The Bible shows that a judgmental attitude toward others is often a coverup for one's own moral weakness: "Therefore you are inexcusable, O man, whoever you are who judge, for in whatever you judge another you condemn yourself; for you who judge practice the same things" (Romans 2:1).

Jesus taught that holy terrorists may be guilty of secret sin even more serious than the faults of those they condemn.

"Why do you look at the speck in your brother's eye, but do not consider the plank in your own eye?" "Hypocrite! First remove the plank from your own eye, and then you will see clearly to remove the speck out of your brother's eye" (Matthew 7:3, 5).

I think the tragic example of televangelist Jimmy Swaggart underscores the truth in Christ's warning. When the PTL scandal broke, Swaggart didn't just cast stones at Jim Bakker. He shot missiles at his fallen fellow minister. And then we learned the shocking truth that Brother Swaggart was himself fooling around with a New Orleans prostitute!

Perhaps unable to conquer sin in his own life, Swaggart found himself lashing out against failure in others' lives. Hypocrisy has always been the heritage of legalism.

Holy weaklings are like the barren fig tree cursed by Christ. They talk about bearing the image of Jesus, but instead they bear the image of the Pharisees who crucified Him. Don't let them put their leash of guilt and fear around your neck.

Legalism is their new leash on life, you know. Sister Stern–type Christians, unable to understand how anyone would obey God simply out of gratitude for salvation, put a yoke of bondage around themselves and others. Without that leash they fear they might run away from the Master. And the truth is, they probably would.

Despite their good intentions, everything legalists do is polluted by appeasement, guilt, and fear. One church elder told me, "Of course I pay tithe. I'd be afraid not to!" Cheap obedience—a big flourish over nothing.

God wants us to cut the leash of legalism and obey Him from a heart set free. "Stand fast therefore in the liberty by which Christ has made us free, and do not be entangled again with a yoke of bondage" (Galatians 5:1).

Never forget it—obedience fueled by appeasing the conscience rather than appreciating Calvary amounts to dead works. "How much more shall the blood of Christ . . . purge your conscience from dead works to serve the living God?" (Hebrews 9:14).

Without question, thousands of zealous Adventists have backslidden into legalism. They have fallen from their first

love, fallen from grace. Their only hope of heaven is to humble themselves at the cross and cry, "Jesus, Son of David, have mercy on me!"

May God save us from the Sister Sterns among us with their dead works. Since these poor people are so pitifully weak, why are we so terribly and totally intimidated by them? Is it because we ourselves are so ignorant of the gospel that we cannot expose their counterfeit?

What should we do about right-wing extremists who try to hold us hostage? Our next chapter deals with church discipline for Khomeini Christians.

---

1. Ellen White, *Evangelism*, p. 190.

Chapter 7

Confronting Khomeini Christians

(Church Discipline for Terrorists)

"God will not be mocked!" warned the Sabbath School superintendent from his power pulpit. "The Lord has shown me that you need to repent!" Pointing his finger around the congregation, he continued, "All of you must humble yourselves and accept the straight testimony!"

This self-styled messenger of the Lord was determined to wipe out worldliness in that little New England church. When anyone ventured a protest against his high-handed tactics or his narrow interpretations of the *Testimonies*, he managed to put them on the defensive:

"So you have a problem with the ministry God has given me? You must be harboring sin in your life. Let's pray together that the Lord will give you a spirit of repentance."

Chastened and intimidated, the victim would usually succumb and kneel for prayer. (We all need prayer, don't we?) Score another victory for fundamentalist terrorism.

Most of our churches are infected by permissiveness, but does that mean we should let Khomeini Christians hold us hostage to legalism? Their solutions are no better than the problems they claim to solve.

In the mountains of Appalachia, where I pastored several small churches, a neighbor woke up one winter morning to

find his water pipes frozen. No problem, he thought, I'll just crawl under the house with my propane torch and melt the ice. He did thaw the pipes in record time. Unfortunately, he also set his house on fire. Only quick action by one of my friends saved the day.

Like the well-meaning man with the propane torch, Khomeini Christians are dangerous. If we let them have their way, they will torch the church. Everyone around them suffers from their wilting criticism. How did they ever get so powerful?

Well, throughout our history, Adventists have had a problem with right-wing extremists. Ellen White constantly pointed such people to Christ and urged Christian charity. Our faithful prophet is no longer with us, and we again find ourselves at the mercy of some of these extremists. Unfortunately, in the past decade or so, things have taken a turn for the worse.

It all began with a crisis in the Adventist Church involving gospel freedom, the investigative judgment, and the authority of Ellen White. Scores of confused pastors and hundreds (perhaps thousands) of lay members abandoned the Adventist fold. Some zealous defenders of the faith blamed this harvest of doubt on what they claimed were seeds sown twenty years earlier by the controversial book *Questions on Doctrine*. These would-be reformers determined to move the church back to "historic Adventism," with a strong emphasis on law and the authority of Ellen White. Fanaticism flourished, and our leaders found no effective way to discourage it.

No doubt about it, "good old Adventism" was back in style. Then we began to pay the price—we had created a monster that could not be satisfied. Some of these Khomeini Christians demanded that all conference policies and programs reflect their narrow-minded legalism. When they didn't get all they wanted, they turned bitter against the church and started tearing it down. Dozens of independent ministries rose up, diverting funds from the church treasury—even tithe funds. (Some of these organizations, of course, do a wonderful work, but many "ministries" are nothing but hotbeds of fundamentalist terrorism.)

Draining off funds from the conference treasury—that's what it took to get the church's attention. Around 1985 our leaders began to realize the crisis that resulted by letting Khomeini Christians have their way. Now we wonder what to do. Should we take the easy way out and give in to their demands? Take the "patient" approach and ignore their excesses? Or should we actively try to help them see the gospel light?

What if they don't want help? Is it ever appropriate to discipline troublemaking Pharisees in order to protect the church body? Let's see what the Bible says about dealing with holy weaklings:

"Receive one who is weak in faith, but not to disputes over doubtful things" (Romans 14:1). So receive them in love, hear them out, try to help them. Put up with their weak scruples—but not with their disputes. Don't let them wreak havoc in the church.

Many pastors and administrators seem resigned to letting Khomeini Christians do their damage, hoping they will eventually run out of steam. They cite the advice of the Jewish sage Gamaliel: "Let them alone; for if this plan or this work is of men, it will come to nothing; but if it is of God, you cannot overthrow it—lest you even be found to fight against God" (Acts 5:38, 39).

Gamaliel's advice is fine in situations where there is a question whether or not the work is of God. But Khomeini Christians leave no doubt that they are doing untold damage. The youth of the church are often alienated. Visitors can be frightened away. The virgin faith of new members is easily corrupted, just as in Christ's day: "Woe to you, scribes and Pharisees, hypocrites! For you travel land and sea to win one proselyte, and when he is won, you make him twice as much a son of hell as yourselves" (Matthew 23:15).

Paul's second letter to the Corinthians contains a stunning exposé of the damage done by Khomeini Christianity. Legalistic Christians known as Judaizers had infiltrated the church with their gospel of merit rather than mercy. Paul actually called them ministers of Satan masquerading as ministers of righteousness.

Let's go to chapter 11 and get the background. We find Paul

grieving over these legalistic teachers who were prostituting the bride of Christ:

> I am jealous for you with godly jealousy. . . . I fear, lest somehow, as the serpent deceived Eve by his craftiness, so your minds may be corrupted from the simplicity that is in Christ. For if he who comes preaches another Jesus whom we have not preached, or . . . a different gospel which you have not accepted, you may well put up with it" (2 Corinthians 11:2-4).

The Corinthians welcomed these Khomeini Christians who corrupted the simplicity of the true gospel. The deceivers did talk about Jesus—but not Christ as our only hope. They preached a gospel, but not the gospel of grace. The church accepted legalism through their influence: "You put up with it if one brings you into bondage, . . . if one strikes you on the face" (verse 20).

Some people don't feel good about worship unless they hear a sermon that brings them into bondage and strikes them with guilt. It makes them feel cleansed to get clobbered by "straight testimony" sermons week after week. Instead of committing themselves to God's grace, they prefer to get "struck on the face" from the pulpit—then go home and live the way they always have.

Paul powerfully condemned the deceivers and their gospel of legalism:

> Such are false apostles, deceitful workers, transforming themselves into apostles of Christ. And no wonder! For Satan himself transforms himself into an angel of light. Therefore it is no great thing if his ministers also transform themselves into ministers of righteousness, whose end will be according to their works (2 Corinthians 11:13-15).

Many Adventists quote this text out of context, applying it to demons masquerading as humans in occult manifestations. We might legitimately draw such a parallel, but it's not the point of the passage. *Paul is referring not to spiritism but to*

legalism. He condemns those who preach a gospel of bondage, calling them ministers of Satan who corrupt the light of God's grace.

Now that's something to think about, isn't it! Something significant indeed.

How strange that people will listen to legalism but reject the messenger of God's good news. Paul constantly had to defend his integrity against the slander of these sinister ministers. They accused him of saying, " 'Let us do evil that good may come' . . . Their condemnation is just" (Romans 3:8). Paul employed emphatic language in defending himself against the charge of preaching cheap grace: "Do we then make void the law through faith? God forbid: yea, we establish the law" (Romans 3:31, KJV).

Paul got quite passionate about people getting tripped up by legalism: "Who is made to stumble, and I do not burn with indignation?" (2 Corinthians 11:29). The Khomeini Christians of Paul's day sought to enforce circumcision as the gateway to their gospel of bondage. Paul expressed an outrageous wish for those who wielded that knife of legalism. "As for those agitators, I wish they would go the whole way and emasculate themselves!" (Galatians 5:12, NIV).

While we might want to tone down Paul's rhetoric, we ought to share his determination to preserve pure gospel faith. Don't you think so? Just as the legalistic Pharisees in Christ's day were "of their father the devil," so it is possible that right-wing extremists of today can be unwitting agents of Satan. We would never tolerate a preacher in the pulpit who tramples upon God's commandments—so why should we tolerate one who tramples upon God's grace?

Jesus set the example for us. First, He patiently tried to help the ministers of bondage. Not only did they refuse the gospel themselves, but they tried to keep others from hearing it. Such oppression called for action. Christ cleansed the temple of their influence. After He put the Pharisees in their place, the children and the lame finally had the freedom to worship God in His house and sing their hosannas unmolested by terrorism.

Not for one moment should we cave in to the demands of

Khomeini Christians and let them torment our youth, new members, and visitors. The apostle Paul stood up to the Khomeini Christians of his day. In the book of Galatians he reports how a conflict arose "because of false brethren secretly brought in (who came by stealth to spy out our liberty which we have in Christ Jesus that they might bring us into bondage), *to whom we did not yield submission even for an hour, that the truth of the gospel might continue with you*" (Galatians 2:4, 5, emphasis supplied).

Thank God for Paul. He wouldn't let the fundamentalist extremists hold hostage new converts and their gospel freedom. His fellow apostle Peter, however, succumbed to political pressure, "fearing those who were of the circumcision [the legalists]. And the rest of the Jews also played the hypocrite with him, so that even Barnabas was carried away by their hypocrisy" (Galatians 2:12, 13).

These legalists had such powerful connections to church headquarters that the apostle Peter himself was afraid of them. No less than noble Barnabas sold out. Paul's act of courage saved the day. He publicly rebuked Peter for opening the door to the legalists, letting them rob new converts of gospel freedom.

Peter and Barnabas were men of personal integrity, but they didn't have the moral courage that Paul displayed in protecting baby believers from being crushed by Khomeini Christians. Peter and Barnabas in their momentary lapse showed the same cowardice as Pontius Pilate, who, for the sake of political interests, pleased the crowd and the entrenched establishment. Truth was crucified in the process. Pilate didn't want to do it, but he lacked the moral courage to just say no!

Standing up for gospel freedom is as politically threatening today as it was back in the early church. Traditionalists acting as right-wing extremists can hold hostage whole churches and even conference executive committees. How many leaders have the courage to act as Paul did?

When politics bears sway over principle, new members and the youth suffer the most. They have no political power base, no vote on the church board or the conference committee. So there are no political penalties for denying them their rights

as fellow citizens of God's family. It's so easy to let Khomeini Christians abuse them—and then put the blame on the victims when they quietly drop out of church. I wonder if what Jesus said about millstones would apply here?

Here's a typical scenario. It's the middle of camp-meeting week. Charles, a wealthy contributor who sits on the conference committee, greets the president outside the cafeteria.

"Hi, Bob. I was walking past the youth tent and couldn't help noticing the music. It was quite loud and had a beat to it. I also heard some hand-clapping going on. Back in my youth we couldn't do those things, and the Lord never changes His standards. Why don't you see if you can do something about the situation out there?"

The president thanks Charles for his interest in the youth and hopes the thing will blow over. But a day or two later they meet again. This time Charles's mood isn't quite as friendly.

"Look, Bob, nothing has changed in the youth tent. I talked to the pastors there myself, and they only defended what they are doing. Not only that, I heard they took the kids out for ice cream after the meeting the other night. Aren't we upholding any of the standards anymore?"

Some presidents at this point go out to the youth tent and pull the plug on the program. Others stand behind their pastors, telling the chronic complainer something like this:

"Charles, your convictions are important to me, but listen. A lot of good things are happening with the youth this week. Several have even recommitted their lives to Christ. So why don't we just let the leaders entrusted with the program do their work as God impresses them? Let's pray for them and leave it at that."

That's usually not good enough for Charles. He might come back with a veiled threat:

"I don't need to remind you, Bob, that next January we will be having our constituency meeting with the election of conference officers. I'm sure the delegates will be looking for evidence of your strong spiritual leadership."

Such threats are familiar to conference presidents everywhere. They present the greatest test of leadership integrity. Will the shepherd sacrifice the lambs of God's flock on the altar of

career ambition? Or will he shun self-interest and risk political suicide for the sake of principle, like the apostle Paul?

Pastors face the same challenge. An ambitious intern, eager to escape Raccoon Hollow and get himself a promotion to Pleasant Valley, will be tempted to play politics. He may pressure a newly baptized housewife to forsake her right to wear a wedding ring just to appease his head elder, whose family has always run the church and who has a red phone hotline to the conference office. But when the pastor knows the president will back him up in doing the right thing, it will be easier to just say no to the power of Khomeini Christians.

Jesus had the courage to resist the spiritual bullies of His day. It's amazing how often He plunged into hot water to save the victims of spiritual oppression.

Consider what happened at the house of Simon, the wealthy and powerful Pharisee. Mary Magdalene came in with her magnificent gift of love, only to be clobbered by criticism. Jesus emphatically defended her: "Why do you trouble the woman?" "Let her alone" (Matthew 26:10; John 12:7). And when the mothers were not allowed to bring their little children to Jesus, He became indignant and stood up for their precious rights.

True leaders will do likewise, no matter what the cost. "The good shepherd gives His life for the sheep. But he who is a hireling and not the shepherd . . . sees the wolf coming and flees; and the wolf catches the sheep and scatters them. The hireling flees because he is a hireling and does not care about the sheep" (John 10:11-13).

How many times our sheep have been scattered—new members and youth chased away from the church—because a hireling pastor didn't stand up to the Khomeini Christians. Notice that the hireling doesn't have anything against the sheep. He probably even likes them, or he would find some other line of work. It's just that he doesn't love them as much as he loves himself.

We hear a lot about reflecting the image of Jesus. That's certainly appropriate, since every true believer yearns for a Christ-like character. Let's remember, though, that Christ was not only the Lamb of God but also the Lion of the tribe of

Judah. I'm convinced that one of the most important qualities of Christ-likeness is to do battle with the wolves who attack the sheep. It's far easier to run and hide than to take a stand and say, "If I perish, I perish!"

Unfortunately, it happens again and again—faithful shepherds who confront powerful legalists suffer politically, while hirelings move up the ladder. Maybe this is one reason "many who are first will be last, and the last first" (Matthew 19:30). God in heaven sees and knows all. " 'Vengeance is mine, I will repay,' says the Lord" (Romans 12:19).

Long ago I asked God not to let powerful weaklings prevent me from conducting a gospel ministry, no matter who might get upset. One of the most difficult stands I've taken involved the baptism of Millie, an elderly lady in the community. She had already been a committed Christian and now wanted to become an Adventist.

There was a problem, though. Blanche, who was Millie's neighbor and one of my members, just didn't think she was ready. Although Millie had studied for months, Blanche was determined that she must read through the *Testimonies* before baptism.

Now, Millie already believed in Ellen White's gift of prophecy. That wasn't enough to satisfy Blanche, who phoned her daily to quiz her on the standards and pronounce her unfit for membership.

Blanche's relentless bombardment was too much. Millie began to get discouraged, wondering whether she ought to be baptized after all.

Well, I couldn't stand by and let the devil destroy Millie through Blanche. Somehow the troublemaker had to be silenced, not just for Millie but for the sake of the whole church—even for Blanche's own salvation. The battle wouldn't be easy, I knew. I had to employ a radical tactic not found in your typical soul-winning manual.

Dropping by unannounced at Blanche's house, I found her eating a bowl of ice cream. She wiped her mouth and launched into a sermon on why Millie shouldn't be baptized.

"Wait a minute," I interrupted. "We've talked enough about Millie. Let's talk about you. Here you are, eating ice cream.

Don't you know we've got counsel about the combination of milk and sugar?"

Blanche flinched. I had only just begun.

"Not only that, I'm sure you've read the *Testimonies* about overeating. How have you gotten so overweight? Are you weak in measuring up to your own standards?"

Blanche's jaw dropped in shock. I wasn't through with her yet.

"Now, you've been a church member about fifty years. How faithfully are you following the straight testimony? I see you have a television here. Tell me honestly. Do you spend your days watching the soaps and game shows? How long has it been since you read through the *Testimonies* yourself?"

The answer came reluctantly, "It's been a while."

"Well, bless your heart," I concluded. "Sounds like you and Millie are in the same boat as all of us. So why don't you quit condemning her and leave her alone?"

Well, Blanche was so mad at me she could have run me out of town. But for the first time in years, she had nothing to say, just as I had hoped. I took advantage of her ceasefire to rescue Millie for baptism.

The day of the baptism, Blanche sat in the back row in the church. When I smiled at her she looked away. So I went right over and gave her a big hug.

"I love you, Blanche. You're not going to stay mad at me, are you?"

I thought I saw the hint of a smile.

Blanche had learned a painful but necessary lesson in humility. What's more, she soon became best friends with Millie and remained so till the day of her death. Millie is still a faithful Adventist, thirteen years after her baptism. Had I not confronted Blanche's legalism, I don't know if Millie would have ever taken her stand.

It's so easy to let the extremists have their way for the sake of peace within the Adventist Church. *But remember, we don't have just ourselves to think about—what about our witness to the world?* Legalism is a disgrace to the reputation of Adventists in the Christian community. For the sake of our evangelism as well as our youth and new members, we must stand

up to the Khomeini Christians among us.

The troublemakers may or may not be sincere. Let's not try to judge their motives; only God can do that. But let's not let them terrorize the flock, either. If we don't do all we can to stop religious terrorists, are we not facilitators of the damage they do?

First, we should patiently explain the truth about God's grace. If that fails, we impress upon them the biblical command to "let each be fully convinced in his own mind" (Romans 14:5). If they still refuse to let others exercise gospel freedom, then it's time to vigorously confront them.

This is not a witch hunt or some kind of gospel inquisition. No, those are the methods used by some Khomeini Christians. Our goal is not to compel them to do things our way but rather to keep them from compelling everybody to do things their way. We don't go looking for trouble, but when trouble rears its ugly head, we must confront it in the name of Jesus Christ.

Through the years in dealing with extremists, I've tried to be kind as well as firm. (After all, they are victims themselves of their own legalism.) We must beware lest we descend to their level of anger when confronting them. This goal of courageous kindness could well be the Mount Everest of Christian leadership.

Such sensitivity to the feelings of holy weaklings, essential as it is, leaves us vulnerable to false guilt. When people get angry at us, we wonder if blame does indeed rest on our shoulders. You see, we've been trained to think along political lines: "If somebody gets mad, you must have said the wrong thing. Learn to keep from offending anyone, like gentle Jesus, meek and mild."

No! Jesus never let people control His ministry. In Matthew 23 He said some pretty bold things to the Khomeini Christians of His day, though He spoke them with tears in His voice. He is our example.

People were angry at Jesus all the time. His own neighbors tried to throw Him over the cliff when His sermon offended their righteousness. One time at camp meeting, some Khomeini Christians tried to do basically the same thing to me,

for the same reason. Six months later they fired their own president, a fine Christian leader.

In standing up to such cruel extremists, we may find that we haven't been as loving as we ought to be. Then we certainly should apologize to the extent of our guilt. But just as important as apologizing for being wrong is resisting false guilt.

In those dark days at the beginning of World War II, Hitler bullied his way across the border into Czechoslovakia. British Prime Minister Neville Chamberlain sought to appease him with a policy of peace at any price. Winston Churchill condemned Chamberlain's courtly cowardice, willing even to wage war in defending freedom. The world still owes him a debt.

The Chamberlains in the church seem so Christ-like. They manage to pacify the Khomeini Christians among us, not realizing that sometimes the most pastoral thing a shepherd can do for his sheep is wage war with the wolves.

May God help us do battle whenever necessary for the sake of protecting the sheep (not protecting our reputation). We must do it kindly and tenderly—but let's do it!

The greatest want of the world is the want of men—men who will not be bought or sold, men who in their inmost souls are true and honest, men who do not fear to call sin by its right name, men whose conscience is as true to duty as the needle to the pole, men who will stand for the right though the heavens fall.[1]

1. Ellen G. White, *Education*, p. 57.

Chapter 8

Day of Wrest and Sadness?

(Keeping the Sabbath Holy)

A delightful book recently came my way: *The Family of God (and How to Live With Them!)*.[1] Author Len McMillan relates a true story that illustrates why we must not take it upon ourselves to dictate the lives of others regarding Sabbath observance:

> My good friend Roger tells about an experience that happened to him while he was a missionary in Africa. They had visitors from the States who were prominent leaders of the world church. After lunch on this particular Sabbath, Roger was heading toward the reef to do some snorkeling. Humming a gospel tune, he walked joyfully along the path with his fins and mask slung over his shoulder. Coming around a turn, he met one of the visiting church leaders. "Where are you going?" inquired the visitor.
>
> "I'm going snorkeling at the reef," replied Roger.
>
> A look of disbelief came into the eyes of the other man as he responded, "You're going snorkeling on the Sabbath?"
>
> Pausing for what must have seemed an eternity, Roger quietly inquired, "What is that you have around your neck?"
>
> "Why, it's binoculars," the man replied.
>
> "What are you going to do this afternoon?" pressed Roger.

76

"I'm going bird-watching," the leader responded.

With a cheery wave Roger started down the path, throwing this closing comment over his shoulder, "Well, I'm going fish watching. Have a happy Sabbath."[2]

We smile at the story, but it brings up some serious questions. What does it mean to keep the Sabbath holy? Should the church enforce a long list of dos and don'ts? And what about married couples making love on the Sabbath—is that participating in forbidden pleasures?

This hot potato of Sabbath keeping has singed the hands of more Adventists than anything else over the last century and a half. Rigid extremists have had a field day asserting themselves as the conscience of the church. Reacting against them, perhaps, some permissive Adventists seem to discard all guiding principles for the Sabbath. And it's sad when God's holy day involves little more than a couple of hours in church away from whatever they feel like doing the rest of the day.

What's the secret of balanced Sabbath keeping? How do we keep God's day holy without making it a day of wrest and sadness?

First, we must get logical about the confused and contradictory regulations we promote. For example, Sabbath School teachers always told me it was a sin to ride my bicycle on Sabbath, even along a wooded nature trail. But a nature ride in the car was just fine. How come? Even a slowly moving car went a lot faster and farther than my bike, so speed itself or distance traveled must not have been the sin. Was it the energy expended that was wrong? No, because a sweat-inspiring hike up the mountain was blessed by pastor and teacher alike.

So what was the problem with my bike ride? No answer was forthcoming. It didn't make sense then, nor does it now. A lot of things about the way we deal with the Sabbath don't make sense.

Swimming in a private cove of Lake Tahoe would be condemned as a mortal sin, but to wade in that same water was OK. There's nothing in the Bible that regulates the water level in which I may dip my body, but good old tradition never fails to speak where God is silent.

When I was a pastor back East, one zealous saint felt it her spiritual gift to police the rest of the church on Sabbath keeping. She let everyone know that she wouldn't pay a ten-cent toll to cross the bridge from Ohio to our church in West Virginia. Instead, she drove way down her side of the river until a toll-free bridge into Kentucky allowed her to keep from defiling the Sabbath with that dime. But would you believe it? I witnessed her using the same dime to purchase a call on the pay phone at church.

Adventists did not invent such senseless scruples. The Pharisees of Christ's day had turned rigid Sabbath keeping into an art form. If strict standards are the essence of Sabbath keeping, then the Pharisees were far more righteous than Christ Himself. Our Lord found Himself condemned throughout the Gospels for what He did on the Sabbath. I wonder how Jesus would have fared in the Adventist churches where I grew up.

Let's take a fresh look into Sabbath rest and seek to find some principles for observing the Sabbath. Come with me back to the Garden of Eden, when God initiated Sabbath rest. He finished creation on Friday afternoon and rested on the Sabbath. Then He invited Adam and Eve to join the celebration of His work—even though they had done no work themselves to earn the right to rest.

Now let us go reverently to Calvary. It's another Friday afternoon, and Jesus once again has completed a work on our behalf. With His dying breath He cries, "It is finished!" Mission accomplished! Mankind redeemed.

As the sun began to set there at Calvary, the friends of Jesus laid Him to rest inside a tomb. There He remained over the Sabbath hours to memorialize His completed work of salvation. After His quiet Sabbath repose, Jesus came forth and ascended to heaven's throne.

Because of the two great accomplishments of Creation and Calvary, Jesus is Lord of the Sabbath. We express our faith in Him as our Maker and Redeemer by sharing the Sabbath rest He earned by His work.

We must understand that nothing more can be added to Christ's work of creation or to His sacrifice on the cross. By keeping the Sabbath, we contribute nothing of our own—we only accept God's gift of life and new life.

The law demands a finished work: "Six days shalt thou labor and do all thy work." But tell me, have you ever finished *all* there was to do when Sabbath came? I haven't, either! Yet we must lay aside our brooms and rakes anyway to find refuge from our unfinished works in the completed work of Jesus.

Complete in Christ—this is the message of the Sabbath. What therapy for legalism! The enemy of souls well knows that many who try to please God wind up trusting in their own works for salvation. I think of how I used to rummage around in my life looking for evidence that I deserved to go to heaven. Then, overwhelmed by my failure to equal Christ's character, I lamented, "Woe is me, for I am undone!"

The Sabbath was designed by God to prevent such spiritual discouragement. Week by week it comforts the conscience, assuring us that despite our unfinished characters we stand complete in Christ. His accomplishment at Calvary counts as our atonement. We enter His rest.

Unfortunately, most of our fellow Christians misunderstand the Sabbath. They consider God's day of rest an ancient Jewish relic with no meaning for modern Christians. Some even regard Sabbath keeping as an attempt to gain salvation by works. Yet nothing could be further from the truth. The word *Sabbath* comes from a Hebrew word meaning to cease, desist, or rest—the very opposite of works.

Of course, works of love are essential in Christian living; it's just that we don't depend upon them for salvation. In appreciation for salvation by grace, genuine faith leads us to be faithful and obedient. You see, we need God's law to convict us of sin—but we are not saved through that law. We're saved by trusting in Jesus. That's the message of the Sabbath!

You may have noticed how the Sabbath commandment differs from the other nine. All the other commandments tell

us what *we* must do for God and neighbor. But the Sabbath points us away from human works—to rest in *God's* work for us. Therein lies our salvation! Without Sabbath rest, our obedience to God would indeed be legalism.

No doubt about it, the Sabbath is the greatest teaching tool of the gospel. It's the brightest of billboards proclaiming Calvary's freedom. Week by week the seventh day comes around to remind us we can't save ourselves—we must trust Jesus. And in this world where atheism abounds, the Sabbath testifies that we didn't evolve by chance. God made us as His children.

One afternoon I had an opportunity to share my testimony informally at California State University, Northridge, near Los Angeles. Ted, a sophomore art student, wanted to know why the Bible insists that he become a Christian.

"Hindus and Buddhists have high moral standards," he argued. "Moslems and Jews worship a personal God. Certainly Jesus was a wonderful man, but couldn't we just appreciate Him as a person and remain outside of Christianity?"

"Here's the difference," I tried to explain. "Many world religions value Christ as a teacher and a worthy example. But only Christianity honors Jesus as the divine Saviour and Creator."

These twin facts of life—creation and salvation—form the foundation of genuine religion, true worship. And God memorialized both of them by the Sabbath, the day of our Lord Jesus Christ.

The book of Hebrews brings us an important warning—it's possible to be a scrupulous sabbatarian without entering Sabbath rest. Chapter 3 sets the stage by recounting the fatal unbelief of those who failed to enter Canaan, followed by a caution for Christians today likewise to avoid falling short of gospel rest. So out of this setting of resting in Christ the Sabbath emerges, when God's "works were finished from the foundation of the world!" and He "'rested on the seventh day from all His works'" (Hebrews 4:3, 4).

Do you see it? We find here two symbols of entering gospel rest: the promised land of Canaan and the Sabbath. The an-

cient Israelites under Joshua finally entered Canaan, yet they still missed the spiritual experience symbolized by that act. And they kept the Sabbath in external form but missed the spiritual experience of Sabbath keeping—gospel rest in Christ.

Several hundred years later, through David, God again called the people of Israel to place their faith in Him (verse 7), but again they refused, and again they failed to enter into His true rest. Did the Jews ever really accept Sabbath rest? Unfortunately not. Both Joshua and David failed to lead them into true Sabbath keeping, so "there remains therefore a Sabbath rest for the people of God" (verse 9).

What Sabbath rest is this which remains for New Testament Christians? "He who has entered His rest has himself also rested from his works, *as God did from His*" (verse 10, emphasis supplied). Now the big question: *When* did God rest from His works? On the seventh day. Verse 4 already told us that. So this same *seventh-day* Sabbath, says the apostle, remains for New Testament Christians to celebrate gospel rest.

What a compelling presentation of Sabbath rest we find here in Hebrews 4! Why, then, do many of us overlook this chapter when attempting to prove the Sabbath? It's because we don't really understand what it means to keep the Sabbath holy. We don't see how the apostle could be telling the Hebrews that their nation never kept the seventh-day Sabbath, when this is exactly the point of the passage.

You see, the Jews—despite their strict observance of the day—missed its meaning. They never entered the gospel rest symbolized by the seventh day. And so they were mere sabbatarians, not genuine Sabbath keepers. Finally they crucified the Lord of the Sabbath, which was total apostasy from Sabbath rest.

I'm wondering whether we sometimes make the same mistake in trying to keep the Sabbath holy. We can be scrupulous about external activities without ever entering Sabbath rest. That's something to ponder carefully.

For a while the early Christians remained faithful to the

gospel and the spirit of Sabbath rest. Soon, however, apostasy began undermining pure faith. Legalism mingled with pagan righteousness by works to corrupt Sabbath rest. The Epistle of Barnabas, written around the year 135, contains the first explicit reference to keeping Sunday. It's interesting to analyze the case presented there for abandoning the Sabbath.

Barnabas argues that Sabbath keeping is impossible. Impossible until the future life in eternity, because in this world all believers are impure and unholy. Barnabas asks, How can we have rest until God's work within our hearts is complete? But in heaven, he states, "we shall be able to treat it [the Sabbath] as holy, after we have first been made holy ourselves."[3]

How very sad! Christians backsliding into legalism thought that Sabbath keeping honors human worthiness. They forgot that the Sabbath takes us away from ourselves to Jesus, to find rest in His accomplishments on our behalf. As the church descended deeper into apostasy, it taught that only perfect Christians, or those nearly so, qualify for sainthood. But according to the New Testament, all who repent of sin and live in Christ are saints in good standing, whatever our imperfections.

Holiness, sanctification, means that we are set apart from the world to live for God. In Genesis 2 we learn the root meaning of the word *sanctify*. God took the seventh day and "sanctified" it, that is, He set it apart from the rest of the week for Himself. In the same way, the Sabbath represents our sanctification. It signifies that God has set us apart from the world to be His people, to enter His rest.

Marriage symbolizes a similar experience. Bride and groom have come apart from everyone else in the world to be joined to each other. They are as much married as they will ever be. Yet now they must preserve their relationship as long as life lasts.

In the Christian life, we come apart from the world to be joined to Christ. We are as much accepted by God as we will ever be. The Sabbath symbolizes this entrance in Christ's rest. Yet day by day we must preserve this "set-apartness," refusing to relinquish our relationship with Jesus during times of

temptation. Therefore sanctification is the work of a lifetime.

But remember, all the time we are growing in Christ we stand "accepted in the Beloved" (Ephesians 1:6), "complete in Him" (Colossians 2:10). In Jesus we are as saved as we will ever be, so long as we don't apostatize.

This is the good news of the Sabbath. It points us away from our unfinished characters to find rest in the finished work of Jesus. Without the Sabbath, we would find ourselves competing with the character of Christ rather than finding refuge in Him, entering His rest. Sabbath rest means refraining from works of salvation—we don't search within ourselves for evidence that God can accept us. Nor do we ask God for help to compete with the character of Christ. Instead, we rest in the finished work of Jesus memorialized by the Sabbath.

We also rest on the seventh day from all pursuit of secular accomplishment: buying and selling anything that pertains to personal gain or business as usual. In fact, we surrender everything that's secular on the seventh day in order to enter God's rest.

Because of all this, the Bible says that the Sabbath is a special sign between God and His people. A sign that He sets us apart from the world to be His children (see Ezekiel 20:12). And He invites us to respond in turn: "Hallow my Sabbaths" (Ezekiel 20:20). That is, "Set the seventh day apart for Me, just as I have set it apart for you. Let's spend that time together each week."

Rearranging our weekend for Sabbath rest may involve some inconvenience or even hardship. Still, we are urged, "Let us therefore be diligent to enter that rest, lest anyone fall after the same example of disobedience" (Hebrews 4:11).

Anytime you take a vacation, you've got to make arrangements with your employer, with your friends and family. Well, the Sabbath is our weekly spiritual vacation. It takes some effort, some diligence, in order to keep that appointment with God.

Yes, we're all busy people. The last thing we may want on Friday afternoon is to set aside our works to rest in Jesus. And that's how the Sabbath tests what is most important to

us. Will we consider what God has done for us worth more than the world offers—more than its business and pleasures, more than news and sports and shopping? Will we take the day off as a spiritual vacation to be with our loved ones—our families, our fellow brothers and sisters in the Lord? Will we rest from the cares of a busy week to worship, to enjoy nature, perhaps to visit the sick and distressed?

Can you see what it means to keep the day holy? The key is to set aside all human accomplishment and secular pursuit for the sake of spiritual rest. Such a time of family and church fellowship requires that we shun business as usual.

Exactly what should we avoid doing on the Sabbath? God has not given us a long checklist of dos and don't like the Pharisees had. Remember the principle involved—avoiding secular accomplishments and activities. Take the television, for example. Some say it's wrong to watch any TV on Sabbath —but what about a commercial-free nature program? And how about religious telecasts? Let us be true to individual conscience, enjoying the blessings of the day while not need-lessly offending weak Christians who major in minors.

Special situations bring us special questions. Nurses and certain other institutional employees must work on the Sabbath. Some suggest that they must turn over to the church all money earned on the Sabbath. But remember that conferences often hire part-time pastors in rural areas whose main duty is conducting Sabbath services. We don't expect them to surren-der their Sabbath earnings. Nor do we expect it of salaried church organists. So why should we put pressure on nurses to surrender Sabbath earnings? "Let each be fully convinced in his own mind," Paul says (Romans 14:5).

Some wonder about eating at restaurants on the Sabbath. They ask, "What's the difference between signing a credit card slip at a restaurant or presenting a ticket at the camp-meeting cafeteria on Sabbath?" Well, what do you think? I believe there are occasional situations that may require buying food on the Sabbath, but normally we can do that other days of the week. Of course, we cannot condemn others for their convic-

tions. Maybe they have doctor's orders, what do we know? One recent Sabbath I went to a drugstore to buy cough medicine for my daughter. I didn't think that was wrong, but I sure hoped nobody saw me tiptoeing into Thrifty's.

Some insist that we should never spend money on the Sabbath. But what about a few dollars to take the kids to the zoo—what better place for city people to enjoy God's nature? I solved the problem by buying a season pass to keep from spending money on the Sabbath. But if such arrangements were impossible, it would not bother my conscience to spend a few dollars on the Sabbath for the sake of opening the book of nature.

Remember that kids need activity—that's the way God made them. Sabbath rest is not rust; there's nothing wrong with them running around in the park. I don't want my kids to play ball on the Sabbath, because a ball is connected to human accomplishment—outscoring an opponent. For them to toss a Frisbee around, though, doesn't involve competition.

You object to children tossing a Frisbee on the Sabbath? Fine. Let each be fully persuaded in his own mind, remember? That doesn't mean we do what we want to do, pleasing ourselves. It says we must do what our individual consciences require us to do to please the Lord.

Does conscientiousness in Sabbath keeping amount to legalism? Not necessarily. Now, if I make the Sabbath a twenty-four-hour tightrope on which to showcase my righteousness and qualify myself for heaven, that's legalism. But if my motivation for keeping the Sabbath holy is gratitude for Christ's great salvation, that's love.

Remember that love is quite particular about works. My wife tries to fix my food exactly as I like it. That's an expression of love for me, not legalism. How sad that some Adventists automatically condemn any conscientious standards as legalism.

We don't want to be legalists, but we shouldn't be *illegalists,* either. Love for God makes us conscientious about keeping His commandments in appreciation for salvation. Love between husband and wife also requires strict diligence in

preserving a good relationship.

Speaking of husbands and wives, what about sex on the Sabbath? As a young pastor I suffered a misunderstanding with some members in my church on that point. Let me tell you what happened.

I had placed a question box in the foyer for the members to write down anything about which they were troubled or just plain curious. Just before the sermon I would reach in and pull out a question to answer. That worked well until the fateful day I found myself answering a question about sex and the Sabbath. Talk about a hot potato!

I suggested that since the Sabbath is a day for family fellowship, it is proper for husbands and wives to enjoy their special fellowship. Their act of love is especially fitting because the marriage relationship symbolizes our relationship with Jesus, Lord of the Sabbath.

I thought I handled it pretty well until I found myself cornered in the foyer after the service. Some of my members were more than a little upset! A couple of days later, a seven-page epistle arrived in my mailbox. Among other things, the writer declared: "I don't let my husband even touch me on the Sabbath." (I frankly wondered if they did much touching during the rest of the week, either.)

The basic objection she had to sex on Sabbath was that lovemaking was pleasurable, and God forbids us from "doing thine own pleasure." She didn't realize that Isaiah 58 also speaks of making the Sabbath a delight. Do we have a contradiction here? What would be the opposite of pleasure? Would misery be the opposite of pleasure? But then how could being miserable be a delight?

Our dilemma is solved when we realize that the word translated *pleasure* in the King James Version is the old English word for secular pursuits. Moffatt's version gives an accurate picture of Isaiah 58:13: "If you refrain from doing your own *business* upon the Sabbath . . ." There is nothing wrong with marriage love on the Sabbath simply because it provides pleasure.

The epistle on sex that woman sent me outlawed lovemaking

on the Sabbath for another reason. She pointed out that several days before giving the law on Mount Sinai, God commanded the men, "Do not come near your wives" (Exodus 19:15).

Why not? We might get an idea by recalling what the refugees from heathen slavery did with sex a few days later—dancing around the golden calf in a wild orgy. Evidently sex was something animalistic to them, something sinful and selfish. Realizing this, God kept them from indulging in their immorality before giving them the law.

But sex isn't immoral or selfish to a loving Christian couple. What do you think Adam and Eve did on the Sabbath their first night together? Can you imagine God warning them, "Now it's going to be Sabbath, so don't get too close to each other. You can hold hands and maybe exchange a quick kiss, but not much more." So there is poor Adam crouched under the waterfalls taking a cold shower, just waiting for the Sabbath to be over.

Ridiculous? Not to some well-meaning extremists among us.

Actually, such fear of sex represents the same medieval thinking that glorifies celibacy when people want to be super religious. I think God has a better way, don't you?

Let's make the Sabbath a delight as the Lord intended. And please pray that I will fulfill the convictions of my own conscience regarding Sabbath-keeping standards—without imposing them upon others in the church.

I've always been intrigued by Ellen White's prediction that near the end of time the people of God will proclaim the Sabbath "more fully." Not just more widely, but more fully—with greater depth and understanding. I hope that time has come.

---

1. Len McMillan, *The Family of God (and How to Live With Them!)*, (Boise, Idaho: Pacific Press, 1988).

2. *The Family of God*, p. 40.

3. Quoted in Samuele Bacchiocchi, *From Sabbath to Sunday* (Rome: The Pontifical Gregorian University Press, 1977), p. 221.

Chapter 9

God of Loving Wrath

(The Moral Influence Theory)

"My God is *not* a murderer!" declared an earnest man I met on my summer camp-meeting tour. "The Lord is my shepherd. He would never think of punishing sinners in hellfire."

Al, a middle-aged businessman from the United States, was visiting friends in British Columbia. He confronted me at the cafeteria and tried to convince me about the new under-standing of salvation that he had recently learned. I had to hurry off to do a meeting, so I had no time to talk that after-noon. Instead, I suggested that we get together that night after my sermon at the youth tent. "We can meet outside your trailer, if you like," I said.

It was past nine when I got up the hill to see him. The sun had already set behind the majestic mountains, but there was plenty of daylight left. Al had a group of five or six friends waiting for me with their Bibles, sitting on lawn chairs in a circle. They listened while Al and I did most of the talking. A pleasant man with sun-bleached hair, he got the discussion going.

"Martin, suppose when you were a child you disobeyed your mother and touched a stove. Did God sentence you to suffer a blister as a punishment for your sin?"

"Of course not," I answered. "He just let me reap the natu-ral result of my disobedience."

"Well," he continued, "does that tell us anything about how sinners perish? We've always been taught that God is punishing them with death—but did you ever consider the possibility that He's just letting them reap the natural result of their disobedience?"

Al waited a moment for that to sink in; then he approached from another angle. "What happens when you cut off a branch from the tree? Does God sentence it to death, or does it simply perish because of being severed from its source of life?"

"I see your point, Al. You believe God lets sinners suffer the death they choose for themselves by living apart from Christ. I agree with that, except to add that He doesn't simply let things run their course. As the Judge of all the earth, He metes out a sentence in harmony with the choices people make."

Al wasn't convinced, so I kept talking: "I like your enthusiasm for God's mercy. But I think you're forgetting His justice."

The others around the circle listened intently as Al responded.

"Martin, God's justice means that He lets things run their course without manipulating our eternal destiny. He doesn't hold back the death that unbelievers have chosen for themselves."

"But wait a minute, Al. The Bible teaches that unrepentant sinners are under condemnation. It says the whole unbelieving world stands guilty before God."

"This concept of condemnation—" Al took a deep breath. "It's just a metaphor, a teaching tool to help us sense our need of grace. God is speaking to us in the language of our guilt and our fears. Because we imagine ourselves under condemnation, God gives us various symbols of salvation so we will no longer be afraid of Him. Actually, the truth is that our kind Father has never held the human race under condemnation."

"So, Al, you're saying that sinners are not under condemnation—they just think they are."

"That's right. They think God's mad at them—that's what keeps them from trusting Him. Jesus came to this world to remove our mental block of unbelief and draw us with His love."

At this point, Al's wife came out with some lemonade. Being thirsty on the warm evening, I emptied my cup quickly. Al kept talking.

"Can you see how Jesus saves us? He sweeps away our doubts and misunderstandings about the Father. That gives us confidence to trust Him and unite our lives with Christ, the source of life."

"But, Al," I protested, "what happened on the cross? Don't you believe Jesus died so we wouldn't have to pay the price of divine punishment for our sins?"

He responded with a question of his own: "Then to whom could such a debt have been paid—to a bloodthirsty Father? The devil? Martin, I'm not trying to put you on the spot, but doesn't it seem rather silly to think that God needs to see some blood shed at the cross before He forgives our sins?"

"Well, doesn't a broken law need legal satisfaction?"

Al smiled. "Do you really think God needs permission from His own law before He can fellowship with sinners? He isn't bound by His commandments. They exist to express His character of love—not as a set of rules that obligates Him to enforce some penalty."

"But didn't Jesus die as our Saviour?"

"Oh, certainly! Christ is our substitute. He died on our behalf, because we could never know God without Calvary's revelation of the Father's love. Besides, through His death we can see the fatal result of being cut off from God. And Jesus died for angels too. Through the cross the unfallen citizens of the universe are able to settle the key question raised in the great controversy between Christ and Satan: Can God be trusted? Jesus revealed to the whole universe the love of God so every creature, human or angelic, will entrust their lives to Him."

"Al, there's a lot of truth in what you're saying," I conceded.

"I'm glad you're catching on," he interrupted with a grin. Al had a sense of humor—a quality I enjoy in anyone I deal with.

"Not so fast, brother," I chided. "You didn't let me finish my sentence. There is a lot of truth in what you're saying, but there's also a good dose of error. It's true that the whole universe benefits from Christ's revelation of God's love, but sinless angels didn't need atonement. They weren't under the wrath of God. The New Testament mentions wrath for sinners

as well as the Old Testament, you know."

"God's wrath is not what we normally think it is, Martin. It's not a sentence of death that He executes. You know that at the cross Jesus suffered the wrath of God. What was that like? Did He cry, 'My God, why are You killing Me!'? No— 'Why are You forsaking Me!' Wrath is being forsaken by a God who reluctantly honors our choice to reject Him."

"What you're saying may sound nice, Al, but it's not kosher Christianity. It's not good Adventist doctrine either. What about the judgment going on in heaven? Isn't Jesus pleading His blood as our mediator in the sanctuary? The Bible says, 'Without shedding of blood there is no remission' [Hebrews 9:22]."

Al took a sip of his lemonade before he replied. "The blood of Christ is a symbol of the loving life He lived on our behalf. Jesus is working with the Father as our mediator—He's not trying to persuade God to accept us. It's the devil that is accusing us—and accusing God Himself, as well. What Jesus is doing is revealing to the entire universe that God has been consistently faithful in all His dealings."

"I can certainly agree that Jesus isn't trying to get God to like us," I interjected. "Who believes that medieval myth anymore?"

Al continued. "In heaven's judgment, God invites the citizens of the universe to review His actions in the great controversy. His sanctuary is cleansed by the clearing away of all misunderstanding about His government. As God is judged worthy of devotion, Satan's challenge is defeated. Finally the wicked are destroyed—not by the flames of a literal hell, but by the revelation of divine glory and the withdrawal of God's sustaining life."

"Al, this idea that hell isn't a real fire to punish the wicked— where do we find it in the Bible? It's got to be biblical."

"You know about the parable of the prodigal son. Did the father have to punish somebody before he welcomed home the repenting boy?"

"No, but he did put the robe around him before welcoming him into the banquet hall. That garment represents the right-

eousness of Jesus Christ, which covers our unworthiness in the judgment."

So the discussion went. (The mosquitoes had their feast too.) By now it was getting so dark we could hardly see each other's faces. It was time to have prayer and go home.

As we rose to leave, Al shook my hand. "Thanks for coming, Martin. Let's both keep studying this out. And be sure to keep in touch."

Several of my best friends believe as Al does about salvation. And I must say that their concept of God appeals to my appreciation of His mercy. For too long Adventists have tended to neglect the sunny side of God's love, His grace toward sinners, focusing instead upon His justice and His wrath against the beast. In trying to escape that emphasis, though, I'm afraid my friends have gone to the other extreme by denying the divine punishment of unrepentant sinners. Reconciling the seemingly opposite attributes of God's love—mercy versus justice—has become a matter of great controversy in the Adventist Church, a real hot potato. At issue is our basic belief about salvation.

The crucial questions are these: What really happened at the cross? Did Jesus die to reveal God's love but not to pay the price of our sin? And at the end of time, does God execute the death sentence upon sinners, or does He simply let them reap the results of their disordered lifestyle?

Adventists like Al, who rejoice in their new concept of God, actually raise more questions than they have answers for. Think about it. If God does not actively punish sin, then it seems we must contrive natural explanations for all judgments against sin throughout the Bible. The seven last plagues, for example, must be ecological disasters. The deaths of Ananias and Sapphira resulted from heart attacks, perhaps. King Herod struck with worms—internal parasites?

Not likely. We cannot escape the biblical picture of a God who actively (though reluctantly) punishes rebellion and hypocrisy. Consider the demise of Moses' enemies Korah, Dathan, and Abiram. More than a timely earthquake, for sure. And remember Lot's wife, turned into a pillar of salt—

hardly the natural chemical result of turning around toward Sodom. The idea that God merely lets sinners destroy themselves collapsed with the walls of Jericho. The whole theory of passive wrath went up in smoke when God destroyed the wicked cities of Sodom and Gomorrah.

Then there's Noah's flood, which didn't just happen. As surely as God punished ancient iniquity, He will punish rebellion when Jesus comes.

I decided to take up Al on his invitation to keep in touch. I called him to point out the compelling biblical evidence that God takes action against sin. He grudgingly acknowledged that Noah's flood had to be an act of God. He said the Lord was simply using the people of Noah's day as an illustration of the death that comes naturally when people hold themselves aloof from Him.

"In other words," I countered, "what you're really saying is that God used the entire antediluvian world as guinea pigs so we can be warned and saved. That wasn't fair to them, was it?"

Al responded: "What really isn't fair is that God would punish His Son for something He didn't do. Even human justice doesn't allow an innocent person to go to the electric chair because of what a criminal did."

"Wait a minute," I said. "Aren't you being inconsistent? You told me Christ died as our substitute—in the sense that we sinners could not have been saved without His loving revelation. Was *that* fair? How could justice permit the Father to abandon His innocent Son so that guilty sinners could know His love?"

Al didn't have an answer, so I pressed the point.

"If the human race couldn't be saved without the revelation of Calvary, why did God destroy the world without giving the victims of the flood the knowledge they needed to be saved?

"Think it through, Al," I urged. "If only a visit from Jesus could teach the way of salvation, God was not fair for keeping millions in fatal blindness by waiting 4,000 years until Calvary before providing the saving revelation of His Son."

Unfortunately, I wasn't able to help Al much. We're still friends, though.

The truth is that God didn't leave the Old Testament people in darkness about salvation. Through the sacrifices, He taught them to put their trust in the blood of the Lamb to come. Some suggest that all this bloodshed misrepresents God as a cruel deity. But who gave Israel the sacrificial system? The pagans? No. God Himself introduced sacrifices for sin at the gates of Eden when He clothed Adam and Eve with the skin of an innocent substitute.

There's a vital and basic difference between Christ's saving sacrifice and the sacrifices of pagan religion. Our God does not demand blood atonement from us—He provided it Himself. We only accept by faith what He offers us in Christ. As our Creator, Jesus had the right to become our Redeemer.

But how can justice permit an innocent substitute to suffer punishment for the guilty? Actually, Christ is more than our substitute. He became one of the human family. As the Son of man, our representative, He took upon Himself the death of the doomed race. He is the second Adam, the new head of humanity. Just as we were lost through the first Adam, we find salvation now through Christ.

Everyone seems to agree that, for one reason or another, Christ died on behalf of the human race. The root question is, Why should God have to sacrifice to Himself? Couldn't He simply overlook sin? The apostle Paul explains: Christ was He "whom God displayed publicly as a propitiation in His blood through faith. This was to demonstrate His righteousness, because in the forbearance of God He passed over the sins previously committed" (Romans 3:25, NASB).

The Bible is plain: God does not want to be unrighteous by passing over sin without punishment, so He offered His Son "for the demonstration . . . of His righteousness . . . , that He might be just and the justifier of the one who has faith in Jesus" (verse 26). You see, the cross explains how He can maintain both justice against sin and mercy toward sinners.

Any confusion about God offering a sacrifice for Himself clears up when we see the dilemma that His sinful children have caused Him. He is not only the tender Father but also the moral governor of His creation. So mercy for sinners and justice against sin

have conflicting claims upon His character of love.

Christian managers know something of this conflict between mercy and justice. All organizations need rules governing operation—chaos results when laws are not upheld. Therefore, rebellion against company law must be dealt with for the good of everyone.

Suppose you have a store policy that no employee can shoplift merchandise—a good law that must be enforced. But there's a poor sales clerk who keeps shoplifting clothes for her baby. You want to show her mercy, but how do you do that without making allowances for others who could argue their own circumstances as an excuse to steal? How do you forgive the lawbreaker without opening the floodgates of lawlessness?

That's God's problem. He solved it at the cross by upholding the penalty required by the law while also providing mercy to sinners.

Let's make no mistake about it. God has a passion for justice. He cares about the oppression in the world—the murder, abuse, greed, and warfare. He reacts against evil; if He refused to act in judgment against it, He would not be a holy God. That's why He declares, " 'Vengeance is mine, I will repay' " (Romans 12:19, NASB).

So there is nothing unnatural about a holy God's wrath against evil. There is vengeance. He will repay.

George Knight of Andrews University recently wrote another of his compelling books, entitled *My Gripe With God*. He quotes well-known writer C. S. Lewis as suggesting that "what most people want is 'not so much a Father in Heaven as a grandfather in heaven—kind of a "senile benevolence." ' We like to think of God as the loving God, the father who unconditionally welcomes back the prodigal son. We don't like to think that we have anything to fear from God." [1]

Knight then shares a personal note: "For 20 years I personally sought to play down and explain away the biblical teaching regarding God's wrath. It wasn't until I began to prepare for writing this book that I was forced to come to terms with the topic." [2]

He became convicted that "God's wrath is not opposed to

His love. Rather, it is an outgrowth of that love. The more love, the more indignation at sin and its results, and thus the more wrath."[3] He explains further:

> Wrath is the natural fruit of divine love. . . . God, as the Bible pictures Him, cannot and will not stand idly by while His creation suffers. *His reaction is judgment on sin, and this judgment should be seen as the real meaning of biblical wrath.* God condemns sin in judgment and will eventually move to destroy it completely. He waits only for the entire universe to acknowledge that He is doing the right thing. Once sin fully matures so that all creation recognizes that God is right in His judgment on sin and sinners, He will react to annihilate both.[4]

Knight then concludes: "The good news is not that God is not wrathful, but that Christ bore the penalty of [God's judgment on] sin for all who believe in Him."[5] Because God could not sacrifice His justice to His mercy, nor His mercy to His justice, in love He took the sinner's just punishment upon Himself by the sacrifice of His Son.

My good friend Steve Mosley writes:

> Did Christ's death on the cross allow God to change from wrath to mercy? No, not in the sense that Jesus persuaded a reluctant Father to forgive. Yes, in the sense that God Himself took the punishment we deserve and was thus enabled to lavish forgiveness on us without denying Himself.
>
> Does God's attitude toward sinners need to change in order for them to be saved? No, not in the sense that He didn't love us before the cross. Yes, in the sense that He had to express His judgment against sin in order to righteously forgive.[6]

Well put, wouldn't you say? Love in justice demands an end to sin, while love in mercy pleads for sinners. God solved this dilemma by providing in His mercy what His justice requires.

The New Testament writers present this gospel in various

symbols. Jesus often likens salvation to the forgiveness of a financial debt. Paul's favorite metaphor is the justification of a defendant in court. He also equates salvation to adoption, the welcoming of an orphan into the family. Peter and others talk of redemption, the ransom paid to reclaim a loved one from capture. And the author of Hebrews compares Christ's work to purification from defilement.

The Old Testament also reveals the cooperation of God's justice and His mercy through the symbolic sacrificial system. Abraham understood that "God will provide for Himself the lamb" (Genesis 22:8). In the Exodus from Egypt, God assured His people, "When I see the blood, I will pass over you" (Exodus 12:13).

From Genesis to Revelation the Bible presents the same gospel: God accepts sinners through the blood of Jesus, our sacrifice. But some Adventists today dismiss the biblical gospel as a mere teaching device having no substance in reality. That's sad.

Figures of speech may vary, but the message remains the same: "Christ has redeemed us from the curse of the law, having become a curse for us (for it is written, 'Cursed is everyone who hangs on a tree')" (Galatians 3:13, emphasis supplied). My friends who deny the gospel also deny God's law the power to condemn the offender. Thus they demote the Ten Commandments to a mere list of suggestions, a policy which God can shove aside to save sinners.

Not surprisingly, their misunderstanding of law and grace also distorts the Adventist sanctuary message. The book of Hebrews teaches that Christ our high priest on behalf of sinners "ever lives to make intercession for them" (Hebrews 7:25). If the gospel consists only of good news about God, what is Jesus doing as He intercedes with the Father? *Is He trying to give God a new revelation of God?*

The counterfeit gospel threatens more than doctrine—our faith in the Bible itself starts skating on thin ice. Think it through—if we dismiss Christ's payment for sin on the cross as merely symbolic, what keeps us from considering His miracles as metaphors too? Is the virgin birth a mere symbol?

Why not? How about the literal week of Creation? The second coming of Christ?

Where do you draw the line?

No wonder God's Word bears this solemn warning: "Even if we, or an angel from heaven, preach any other gospel to you than what we have preached to you, let him be accursed" (Galatians 1:8). We had better not tamper with the truth about the cross. In denying Christ's saving sacrifice, I'm afraid my friends have invented a false gospel that is accursed.

Like all heresies, though, their false gospel contains elements of vital truth. For too long some of us have imagined our Father to be frowning at our failures. We need to see His friendly face. We must serve Him for appreciation of His love rather than from fear of His damnation.

I can think of no better way to conclude this chapter than with Ellen White's simple and eloquent description of the gospel.

> Faith is the condition upon which God has seen fit to promise pardon to sinners; not that there is any virtue in faith whereby salvation is merited, but because faith can lay hold of the merits of Christ, the remedy provided for sin. Faith can present Christ's perfect obedience instead of the sinner's transgression and defection. When the sinner believes that Christ is his personal Saviour, then, according to His unfailing promises, God pardons his sin, and justifies him freely. The repentant soul realizes that his justification comes because Christ, as his substitute and surety, has died for him, as his atonement and righteousness. . . .
>
> The law demands righteousness, and this the sinner owes to the law; but he is incapable of rendering it. The only way in which he can attain to righteousness is through faith. By faith he can bring to God the merits of Christ, and the Lord places the obedience of His Son to the sinner's account. Christ's righteousness is accepted in place of man's failure, and God receives, pardons, justifies, the repentant believing soul, treats him as

though he were righteous, and loves him as He loves His Son. This is how faith is accounted righteousness.[7]

1. George Knight, *My Gripe With God* (Hagerstown, Md.: Review and Herald, 1990), p. 37.

2. *Ibid.*

3. *Ibid.*, p. 39.

4. *Ibid.*, p. 40, emphasis suppplied.

5. *Ibid.*

6. Steven Mosley, *Channels* (Summer 1988), p. 9.

7. Ellen White, "Christ the Way of Life," *Review and Herald*, November 4, 1890.

Chapter 10

What About Ellen White?

(The Spirit of Prophecy)

Right from the start let me clarify my personal convictions about the Spirit of Prophecy in our church. I have full confidence that Ellen White served God as a prophetic messenger to Seventh-day Adventists. I believe her writings provide a continuing and authoritative source of inspiration to us. Furthermore, I am willing to accept that whatever she wrote on religious matters was inspired by the Holy Spirit.

Does that mean her books and articles reveal no growth in her understanding of truth?

Don't answer that too quickly.

Adventists all recognize Ellen White's vital role in our history, but convictions vary about how the church today can benefit from her spiritual gift. You can find two extremes in the church—those who ignore or downplay her counsels and those who enthrone her as lord of God's Word. Let's search for a position of balanced truth.

Ellen White herself had no doubt about her calling. Fearlessly and faithfully she rebuked, comforted, and counseled. But it's interesting that she refused the role of a theological referee. She reminded church leaders that the Bible is our final authority, not her writings: "We should make the Bible its own expositor."[1] Yet some Adventists find it difficult to accept what the Bible says until

they hear an Amen from Ellen White.

I remember an experience I had conducting a witnessing seminar in the Chicago area. I was explaining that Jesus must be the center of every Bible study lest we err like the Pharisees did. Christ accused them of searching the Scriptures to find eternal life, yet refusing to come to Him, the object of the Scriptures, in order to receive that life. I noted that the King James Version doesn't accurately represent the meaning of John 5:39, because it says Jesus told the Pharisees to "search the scriptures"—when obviously they already were searching the Scriptures while rejecting Christ.

Immediately a man's hand shot up. "Pastor, the Spirit of Prophecy used that text in the way you say it shouldn't be. In the *Testimonies* she quotes John 5:39 exhorting someone to read the Bible, to 'search the Scriptures.' Do you think you know more about that text than the servant of the Lord does?"

Well, it was an awkward moment for me. Fortunately, I had been reading *The Desire of Ages*, where Ellen White quotes John 5:39 the opposite way—making the very point I was trying to get across. I identified the chapter where our brother could look it up and see for himself.

I'm sure he finally accepted the true meaning of the text when he realized Ellen White endorsed it. But the Bible by itself wasn't good enough for him. He rejected the principle of *sola scriptura*—the Bible and the Bible only.

But some would ask, "In what sense is the Bible our *only* rule of faith and practice? The laws of the land, employee handbooks, the *Church Manual*, and countless other documents are rules of practice." True, but all these are authoritative only in the sense that they reflect the principles of God's Word. Corporate policies and even civil laws are not in themselves eternal absolutes. The Bible stands unique as a law unto itself, the standard by which all lesser authorities must be tested.

At this point you may be thinking: "If the Bible can be understood without the gift of prophecy, why do we need Ellen White's books at all?" Notice this inspired answer:

The written testimonies are not to give new light, but to impress vividly upon the heart the truths of inspiration already revealed. Man's duty to God and to his fellow man has been distinctly specified in God's word, yet but few of you are obedient to the light given.[2]

Little heed is given to the Bible, and the Lord has given a lesser light to lead men and women to the greater light.[3]

Whatever we need to live for God we can find, explicitly or implicitly, in the Bible itself. Now, God's Word doesn't specifically condemn tobacco, but it does teach the "body temple" principle. And how about cocaine? Do we need yet another prophet to tell us we must "just say no"? Not when we have biblical principles to guide us.

Well, then, what is the authority of a prophet? Merely pastoral? No, much more. Pastors and teachers receive their instruction through studying the Bible. Prophets, on the other hand, receive direct inspiration from the Spirit outside the written Word. One would expect a direct revelation from God via a vision to be more reliable and authoritative than an indirect revelation received through personal study. Even so, prophetic messages must still be tested by the Bible.

A friend of mine served as a missionary in Korea. I can assure you he is more authoritative than I am in interpreting that language. I have only indirect access through an English-Korean dictionary, while he's had the benefit of direct dialogue with Koreans. Even so, despite his inside information, my friend's word is not final. Everything he says in Korean must be tested by the same authority available to anyone who can read the dictionary.

In the same way, prophets, despite their direct connection with heaven, must submit their messages to the Scripture test. That is, unless you want confusion in the church.

During the first campaign I held as an evangelist, one of our visitors invited me to attend a nondenominational prayer meeting. It turned out to be a charismatic praise service. I sat

there amazed as person after person jumped up with a prophetic message to bind the conscience of different ones in the audience. They even spoke for God using the first person, such as: "Thus saith the Lord, 'I want John to sell his new car and be satisfied with a used one.'"

As you can imagine, the will of the Lord became confusing. Those people needed some final authority to rule above their spiritual gifts. No wonder the New Testament encourages us to put latter-day prophets to the test:

"Do not despise prophetic utterances. But examine everything carefully; hold fast to that which is good; abstain from every form of evil" (1 Thessalonians 5:20-22, NASB).

Consider the Bereans. Paul was a prophet, yet the people of Berea did not accept anything he said without proving it for themselves by Scripture. Paul did not consider this doubting. He said they were noble.

Many seem reluctant to be good Bereans by testing prophetic messages. It's hard to examine truth for oneself. Human nature finds it so much easier to default on responsibility and simply take everything the preacher or the prophet teaches as gospel. But the Word of God is clear—regarding "prophet utterances," we must "examine everything carefully." Time and place must be considered.

But isn't this testing process mere presumption? Can we pick and choose what is inspired and what isn't? No, certainly we cannot pick and choose what we want. When the instruction of a preacher or prophet is validated by the Bible, we must pick up the cross even if it has splinters. We test by the Word and not by the flesh.

So spiritual gifts must be judged by the Word, never the other way around. As Paul said, "The spirits of the prophets are subject to the prophets" (1 Corinthians 14:32).

Ellen White herself emphasized that "the Bible is to be presented as the word of the infinite God, as the end of all controversy and the foundation of all faith." [4] And here once again, she emphatically places her writings beneath the greater light of God's Word. What else could we expect from a true prophet?

Some Adventists, despite their sincere desire to properly uphold the Bible, manage to make Ellen White their final authority. How do they manage this? Through circular reasoning:

"Why do I believe in Ellen White? Because everything she says agrees with the Bible. So everything in the Bible can be tested by her writings. I rely upon her interpretation of Scripture. This means that in principle I accept 'the Bible and the Bible only,' since everything she says agrees with the Bible."

A Catholic friend of mine uses similar reasoning: "Why do I believe whatever the pope says? Because everything he says agrees with the Bible. So everything in the Bible can be tested by the teachings of the pope (including Sunday worship). I rely upon his interpretation of Scripture. This means that in principle I accept 'the Bible and the Bible only,' since everything the pope says agrees with the Bible."

You see the problem. *Anything that defines Scripture threatens to replace it as the final authority.* The fundamental issue of the Protestant Reformation was that the Bible must be its own interpreter. It was not that the pope was a bad interpreter of Scripture and now we must find a better lord over the Word. Remember, the Bible itself is its own final word. It contains the entire system of truth.

Some suggest that since Ellen White proved herself to be God's messenger in the 1840s, ever afterward—for the next seven decades—everything she taught must, without question, be the word of God. Having once been proven faithful to the Scriptures, never again need she be tested by the Bible. This sounds like "once saved, always saved" for prophets.

We find examples in Scripture where prophets wandered away from God's will. Ellen White, of course, remained faithful throughout her long ministry. Yet still, as a matter of principle, should we not test all her writings by the Word? At what point could we pronounce her beyond the need of testing, having become, in fact, once saved, always saved?

"Once saved, always saved"—every good Adventist ought to flee in horror at the very hint of such heresy. Don't you think?

Perhaps some of us invoke the doctrinal authority of Ellen White to escape the bother of Bible study: "Sister White taught the importance of health reform, and that settles it for me!"

Sounds good. Was the gift of prophecy given to make us lazy? I wonder whether some of Ellen White's most vocal supporters understand what she really taught. Like the Pharisees with Moses, do they defend their prophet zealously but ignorantly?

Something to think about. We need to get our understanding of inspiration back on solid ground.

Consider our roots in the Millerite movement. We Adventists believe that the advent awakening was inspired by God, even though the movement mistakenly predicted Christ's coming on October 22, 1844. (The first-century disciples suffered disappointment in their expectations when Jesus died and was buried in the tomb—even though God was leading their movement.) Let's also think about Martin Luther. He was led by God to launch the Protestant Reformation although he held a number of doctrinal errors, such as eternal hell and Sunday sacredness. Then there's John the Baptist, actually an inspired prophet, proclaimed by Christ Himself as the greatest of all prophets—yet he erroneously expected a political Messiah to chase out the pagan Romans who occupied the Holy Land. Jesus performed the opposite of his expectations until at last the prophet even doubted that He was indeed the Saviour: "Are You the Coming One, or do we look for another?" (Matthew 11:3).

Not only was the prophet completely mistaken about how Christ would come, but his movement also suffered from legalism. His disciples hoped "to be justified by the works of the law."[5] Yet despite such serious misconception, John was God's chosen prophet, inspired to herald the Messiah.

Did the prophet's imperfect doctrine disqualify him from being God's messenger? Jesus didn't think so. John fulfilled his divine mission of announcing the Messiah. Then why did God permit him to preach immature theology along with truth?

The prophet had to teach on the kindergarten level. God's people were not ready for the full message, so He gave them a prophet who could *meet them on their own level and lead them* where they finally could appreciate the gospel. God never intended for John to preach with the identical insights that Paul introduced later on. The people were not ready for Paul's lofty gospel. So God called a prophet who shared many of their misconceptions so they could relate to his teaching.

Here's the point: If we accept Christ's testimony that John was a prophet in spite of his need for theological growth, what about Ellen White? Why should we expect more from her than we do from the greatest of the prophets?

The fact is that in spite of inspiration, Ellen White initially held a number of convictions that later changed as the Holy Spirit guided her understanding. This should only be expected, as she herself explained: "That which God gives His servants to speak today would not perhaps have been present truth twenty years ago, but it is God's message for this time."[6]

One example of this is how, back in the 1850s, she counseled a brother not to forbid the eating of pork.[7] It wasn't until her health visions in the 1860s that she took a stand on unclean meat. Evidently the Lord was leading in a gradual way.

Another area of growth in Ellen White's understanding is her concept of God's character. Notice this from her *An Appeal to the Youth*, published in 1864:

God loves honest-hearted, truthful children, but cannot love those who are dishonest.

The Lord loves those little children who try to do right, and He has promised that they shall be in His kingdom. But wicked children God does not love . . . . When you feel tempted to speak impatient and fretful [sic], remember the Lord sees you, and will not love you if you do wrong.[8]

Now compare the above with the following, written twenty-eight years later (after 1888):

Do not teach your children that God does not love them when they do wrong; teach them that He loves them so that it grieves His tender Spirit to see them in transgression.[9]

Thank God, Ellen White was always moving in the right direction. Suppose that in 1864 she had taught that God loved bad children, then later said He didn't love them—that would be a problem. But the growth in her understanding of truth proves that she was led by the Spirit of truth.

It has been an agonizing struggle for many Adventists to acknowledge the reality of Ellen White's need to grow. But why? If we see immaturity and growth in the greatest of the prophets, can we not accept them in our own? Just think. What if God had given the message of 1888 to us in 1844? We couldn't have digested it. It was hard enough to swallow forty-four years later.

Since Ellen White was indeed a true prophet, should we not expect to see a pattern of growth in her writings to correspond with the growing capacity for maturity in our movement?

Ellen White also may have grown in her understanding of prophecy. Back in the first edition of *The Great Controversy,* she wrote that Babylon "cannot refer to the Romish Church, for that church has been in a fallen condition for many centuries."[10] But in her 1911 revision she inserted a significant word: Babylon "cannot refer to the Roman Church *alone*, for that church has been in a fallen condition for many centuries."[11]

Compare these two sentences: "The pastor did not rob the bank." "The pastor did not rob the bank *alone*." Do you see the difference made by that one little word?

It doesn't matter to me whether this change in wording reflects a transition in Ellen White's understanding of doctrine, or whether she was revealing a new dimension in what she already understood. The simple fact is that her 1911 position can more easily be defended from the Bible. That should inspire our confidence!

During the doctrinal controversy in 1888, Ellen White did indeed question her previous position on the law of Galatians. Utterly dismayed at the unchristian attitude of those defending the traditional Adventist position, she testified: "For the first time I began to think that it might be we did not hold correct views, after all, upon the law in Galatians, for the truth required no such a spirit to sustain it."[12]

Although Ellen White had previously supported the traditional view,[13] now, as always, she was willing to walk in the light. This concerned some of the brethren, who wanted to settle the discussion by a manuscript she had once written. Here is her reply: "Has he [Waggoner] not presented to you the words of the Bible? Why was it that I lost the manuscript and for two years could not find it? God has a purpose in this. *He wants us to go to the Bible and get the Scripture evidence.*"[14]

In this highly significant statement, Ellen White realized God had purposed that her manuscript be lost to force the group to settle their questions from the Bible alone. They were not to use her writings to nail down their interpretation of Scripture. She repeated this position a few years later in the controversy over the "daily" in Daniel 8.[15]

Another clear example of doctrinal growth is Ellen White's understanding of the Holy Spirit. Ellen White's rich and mature understanding, so beautifully expressed in her later writings, is entirely absent in the first five decades of her ministry.

Either the Holy Spirit changed from an impersonal force to a real person in the year 1896, or Ellen White reversed an incorrect doctrinal position. I think we know the answer—and once again we see the Lord's leading.

What about righteousness by faith? Did Ellen White mature in her understanding of salvation? If she did, how can we know the final truth about the gospel?

We need have no uncertainty. God nailed down the truth about righteousness by faith long before the days of Ellen White. The apostle Paul proclaimed by inspiration: "Even if we, or an angel from heaven, preach any other gospel to you than what we have preached to you, let him be accursed" (Galatians 1:8).

That settles it. What we find in the book of Galatians is the gospel's eternal benchmark. Not even an angel from heaven could change the established Word of God.

Some among us believe that Ellen White added some new element of the gospel to lay an extra burden on the final generation. How could that be, though, in the light of the warning we just read? Beyond that, keep in mind the verse we quote to our Protestant friends who say that the salvation covenant was amended to permit Sunday keeping: "Just as no one can set aside or add to a human covenant that has been duly established, so it is in this case" (Galatians 3:15, NIV).

You see, once the salvation covenant was confirmed at Calvary, nothing could be changed or added to it. Not even by an angel from heaven in 1888.

So why not study the Bible itself to understand the gospel? Don't believe the medieval falsehood that God's Word is so complicated it can't be understood without an interpreter. Remember that Ellen White declared the Bible to be its own expositor. Let's also keep in mind what she said about the greater light of the Bible ruling her own lesser light. That means I don't need permission from Ellen White to believe what God settled long ago in the Bible. And I'm not going to cast aside my assurance of salvation and cower in fear every time the extremists try to scare me with their favorite quotations.

So when we read in Ellen White that we can't be saved unless we reflect the image of Jesus fully, we must interpret that in the biblical sense of perfection: Because Jesus lived a life of uncompromised faith commitment to the Father, I must by faith reflect that attitude. And when Ellen White says we can't be sealed with even one spot on our characters, again we interpret that in the biblical light that God requires an uncompromised faith commitment, withholding nothing from Him.

We will always trust in the merits of Christ for our salvation. Even after probation closes, it's the blood of Jesus on the doorpost of my faith that saves me from death.

So here's the key to a conscience that is clean before the Lord: Salvation comes to my unworthy soul by the mercy of God. The Bible says it, I believe it, and that settles it for me.

Does such a firm affirmation of God's Word make you a little nervous? Why? Ellen White was not afraid of the Bible, even when it challenged her previous beliefs. She humbly testified:

> The Lord has been pleased to give me great light, *yet I know that He leads other minds, and opens to them the mysteries of His Word*, and I want to receive every ray of light that God shall send me, though it should come through the humblest of His servants.[16]

This willingness to accept new light disturbed certain church leaders. They refused to believe prophets could change their minds and mature in their teaching. But the fact is that inspiration is perfect for God's purposes, not necessarily our own. He reveals truth in His own time and way. That's one of the reasons Ellen White insisted we test everything she wrote by the Bible.

Consider this. If we fail to test Ellen White's messages by the Bible and make her an infallible law unto herself, what could prevent some new prophet from intruding into the sacred circle of scriptural authority?

This question is more than a mere possibility. Back in the 1890s a curious crisis arose in the church when Anna Phillips Rice appeared on the scene. She claimed the same prophetic gift Ellen White had—and she actually won endorsement from some of our most influential church leaders. A. T. Jones held up her testimonies before a church assembly, proclaiming the new "prophet" to be just as inspired and therefore just as authoritative as Ellen White. Fortunately, Ellen White herself, in Australia, caught wind of the crisis and put an end to Anna's fledging ministry.

What if another Anna Phillips Rice appeared today? *It's happening!* In the Adventist Church today, well over a dozen members claim to have inherited Ellen White's mantle of

prophetic authority. On a recent camp-meeting circuit, I was confronted with several of them. Someone reverently handed me a thick manila folder full of "prophetic counsels" she valued on a par with Ellen White's books and the Bible.

Can you imagine the chaos in the church if large numbers of our members welcomed a new prophet as having equal authority with Ellen White and the Bible and forcing everything we believe to be reinterpreted by this new revelation?

If we were to grant Ellen White the power to reinvent Bible truth, then every succeeding prophet would have to have the same authority. There would no longer remain any objective anchor for our faith. Our only safeguard is the Bible—we must test by God's Word everyone who claims the prophetic gift, including Ellen White.

God save us from such a day! But the test will come; of that you can be sure.

You know, the tombstones of those who have exaggerated the gift of prophecy line the hallway of Adventist history. Defectors from our chruch usually make their first mistake in putting Ellen White above the Bible. When their impossible expectations of her ministry are shattered by reality, they feel devastated. Bitterly they reproach our prophet and abandon our church. I personally know several dozen former Adventists who have had the same tragic experience.

How much pain we suffer through misconceptions about inspiration! Not only that, our witness to fellow Christians is severely compromised if we promote unauthorized claims about Ellen White.

You know how it goes. Your Baptist friend down the street finally agrees to attend church with you. Unfortunately, before she ever hears an Adventist sermon, what happens in Sabbath School shakes her confidence in our message. Too often, all she hears is, "Sister White says this, Sister White says that." So she leans over to you and whispers, "All this talk about Sister White—what about the Bible!"

You've lost her. She brands the Adventist Church a cult and never comes back. Who will give account for her soul?

To avoid such heartbreaking situations, many pastors encourage Sabbath School superintendents and teachers to be discreet about invoking the authority of Ellen White. But tell me—Is the real solution to hide what we believe about the Spirit of Prophecy? Or do we need to get our thinking straight and put the Bible first and foremost?

When we establish ourselves as truly people of the Book, we can quote Ellen White without repelling informed Christians. Many of them already know about spiritual gifts and will be delighted to welcome Ellen White in her proper prophetic role. But we must meet them on the solid rock of the Bible only as our rule of faith.

I ask you, Which Adventist doctrine cannot stand on the Bible alone? Despite such a solid biblical base, some Adventists perceive *sola scriptura* to be a threat to the authority of Ellen White. Often they recite the following warning of inspiration: "The very last deception of Satan will be to make of none effect the testimony of the Spirit of God . . . . Satan will work ingeniously . . . to unsettle the confidence of God's remnant people in the true testimony."[17]

Is this ingenious deception happening right now? I see two basic attacks against Ellen White's authority. Many despise her writings in order to "do their own thing," speeding along the highway to heaven in reckless abandon. Will they be lost for rejecting Ellen White? Only because her straight testimony that they refuse is based upon the Bible.

False freedom is a dangerous temptation indeed. But Satan has reserved his most cunning deception for those who are blindly zealous for Ellen White the way the Pharisees were for Moses. Were the Millerites perfect in their theology? Even the prophet John was not flawless in his teaching. Then why must Ellen White be?

We need enough faith to look past her humanity and see God at work in her gift. Otherwise our appreciation of inspiration will be so shallow that we must deceive ourselves to retain our "faith."

Where would the Adventist Church be without Ellen White? Less enriched, for sure—but would we have no hope?

Some insist that Adventism will collapse unless we build our faith on her writings. But is Ellen White the rock on which Christ built His church?

Tragically, Ellen White's friends have done much more damage to her reputation than her enemies. Really, she doesn't need us to defend her—she only needs to be read in her proper relation to the Bible. Any genuine believer will recognize in her writings the voice of the Shepherd.

---

1. Ellen G. White, *Testimonies to Ministers*, p. 106.

2. ———, *Testimonies for the Church*, vol. 5, p. 665.

3. ———, *Selected Messages*, book 3, p. 30.

4. ———, *Christ's Object Lessons*, pp. 39, 40.

5. ———, *The Desire of Ages*, p. 276.

6. ———, *The Ellen G. White 1888 Materials*, "Talk to Ministers," p. 133.

7. ———, *Testimonies for the Church*, vol. 1, pp. 206, 207.

8. ———, *An Appeal to the Youth* (Battle Creek Mich.: Steam Press, 1864), pp. 42, 62.

9. ———, *Signs of the Times*, February 15, 1892.

10. ———, *The Great Controversy* (1888), p. 383.

11. ———, *ibid.* (1911, emphasis supplied).

12. ———, *Manuscript 24*, 1888.

13. ———, *Sketches From the Life of Paul* (Washington, D.C.: Review and Herald, 1974 facsimile reprint), p. 192.

14. Quoted in LeRoy E. Froom, *Movement of Destiny* (Washington D.C.: Review and Herald, 1971), p. 229, emphasis supplied.

15. *Selected Messages*, book 1, p. 164.

16. Quoted in Froom, p. 230, emphasis supplied.

17. Ellen G. White, *Review and Herald*, February 24, 1874.

Chapter 11

Is the Church Going Through?

(Laodicea and the Remnant)

"No matter what happens, the Seventh-day Adventist Church is going through!"

We often hear such ringing proclamations of denominational patriotism, especially when confronted with problems in the church. And all loyal Adventists feel like shouting a fervent "Amen!" An important question comes to mind, however. What do we mean by "the church" that is "going through"?

Do we mean that God will preserve a remnant in the last days who keep His commandments and have the faith of Jesus? Or do we imagine that the Seventh-day Adventist organization is guaranteed a once-saved, always-saved status?

It's amazing how many Adventists have no assurance whatever in personal salvation—they don't even believe in it—yet they proclaim once-saved, always-saved for our organizational structure. As one man told me, "Even if the General Conference president and I are the only ones left in the church, I'm staying with the ship."

Wait a minute. What is the "ship" of salvation? Merely having our names recorded on the books of the Seventh-day Adventist Church? Or is it the gospel of Jesus Christ in the context of biblical truth?

114

Many Adventists, caught up in blind denominational patriotism, have forgotten the principles of conditional prophecy. Obedience to God's covenant has always been the condition of salvation. And that goes for organizations as well as individuals. So how can we insist that it is *impossible* for our church to forfeit favor with God, no matter what we do?

The arrogance of such a statement is exceeded only by its ignorance. Do we imagine ourselves immune from the rejection suffered by the Jewish nation—God's chosen people—when they rejected the gospel?

Right here I want to affirm my personal appreciation for the leaders of integrity God has given to our church. How pitiful that we tend to criticize them more than we pray for them. If we could look past our own limited perspective and see the multifaceted dimensions of the problems with which our leaders wrestle, we would cherish a greater appreciation for what they are doing.

Thank God that many of our leaders do have top-notch talent and untarnished commitment to Christ. Let's not allow the things that are wrong to keep us from rejoicing in all that is right about our church.

That's not to say that our leadership and church structure have no flaws. Many bureaucrats in their ivory towers have been so long isolated from the real world of soul-winning that they appear incapable of giving wise direction to church programs. Some of these seem totally out of touch with the 1990s. It may have been a decade or more since they personally led anyone to Christ.

Such ineffective leadership, though tragic, is not a problem unique to Adventism. All organizations, over time, tend to neglect the painful but vital work of pruning needless foliage.

Nevertheless, there are marvelous things happening in the Adventist Church. In most of the world we see dramatic growth. Here in North America we have a number of exciting and effective outreach projects. I'm particularly enthusiastic about new dimensions in our media outreach (pardon my bias—I work at the Adventist Media Center). Member-

ship is increasing among Blacks and Hispanics, but Anglo growth has stalled—deaths and desertions may actually exceed baptisms. (Exact figures are difficult to obtain since conference baptismal reports do not segment new members by ethnic background.)

Here's what one of our North American church leaders tells me: If we define an active Adventist as a member who attends at least once a month, then Anglos are probably losing members here. That would mean that the majority of the church in North America is moving backward.

I find that downright alarming, don't you? We need the courage to confess and confront reality. But some are going so far as to say the church has become Babylon. That has definitely not happened, as we will see proven from the Bible later in this chapter.

Nevertheless, our church right now is in a state of real need. While our songs and sermons insist that we want Jesus to return, actually it seems we are no more eager for Christ to come than for barbarians to come and invade our prosperity. Such is the spiritual state of North American Adventism. We don't smoke, but we're not on fire. We don't drink, but we refuse to be under His influence. We don't dance, but neither do we delight in His salvation.

This lethargic attitude causes our Lord to lament: "I know your works, that you are neither cold nor hot. I could wish you were cold or hot" (Revelation 3:15).

We Adventists have long recognized the relevance of this rebuke to our own generation. We could be rejoicing in the New Jerusalem but instead are languishing in Laodicea. Being selfish and indolent, we are yet somehow proud of ourselves for possessing the pillars of truth.

We must yet learn the truth within the truth. Like the Pharisees of old, are we zealous sabbatarians who have resisted Sabbath rest? We know where the dead are, but we have not been alive in Christ. We accept the sanctuary doctrine, but we ignore the daily intercession of our Priest. We talk of His soon return, yet we live as if He never will.

In 1888 our church received a wake-up call with the proclamation of Christ's righteousness. Still we slumber, more than a century later. Yet the pillars of our truth remain. And since this is the only denomination that has claimed those pillars of truth, we are indeed the fold God seeks to prepare for His sheep from Babylon. No question about it. Enfeebled and defective though we be, we are still God's movement of destiny. But where do we go from here?

Ponder this dire warning from Jesus: "So then, because you are lukewarm, and neither cold nor hot, I will spew you out of my mouth. . . . Therefore be zealous and repent" (Revelation 3:16, 19).

Strange words coming from our loving Lord. I used to cringe at the thought of being "spewed out," that is, "spit out," by Christ. It seemed crude, even cruel. Then one day I noticed that the word *spewed* actually should be translated *vomit*. This represents involuntary expulsion, not disgusted rejection.

You see, our lukewarm love nauseates Jesus. While this is not a pretty picture, at least we can find comfort in knowing that Christ does not want to expel us. It's just that our neutrality makes Him sick.

Thank God, there's still hope. The warning to Laodicea closes with a heart-touching invitation to His lukewarm lovers and a glorious promise for eternity: "Behold, I stand at the door and knock. If anyone hears My voice and opens the door, I will come in to him and dine with him, and he with Me. To him who overcomes I will grant to sit with Me on My throne, as I also overcame and sat down with My Father on His throne" (verses 20, 21).

Seventh-day Adventists have here a wonderful, glorious promise if we, its members, repent, but a fearful threat if we refuse to get down to business with God. Where will we go from here? One thing is certain. Jesus wasn't bluffing when He threatened to reject Laodicea. Ellen White recognized this when she warned in 1888 that "if the Church should go into darkness *the Lord would raise up others to finish the work— that He had agents that He could call into action at any moment.*"[1]

Our organization is not once-saved, always-saved anymore than the Jewish organization was. We can learn a lot from the history of God's chosen nation. In fact, by looking at their past, we see a forecast of our own future, a dramatic preview of end-time events.

Come with me to Mount Sinai, where the ancient Israelites danced around the golden calf. Only days before God had saved His people in the Exodus, yet apostasy quickly undermined true worship.

Things became worse as the centuries passed. King Solomon, the very one who built God's temple, defiled Jerusalem with paganism. As time went on, the apostasy deepened. Faithful prophets urged the people to reverence the One who had created them and saved them from bondage. Isaiah and others pointed to the Sabbath, urging God's chosen ones to enter His rest. Yet they persisted in worshiping the sun and the "works of their own hands" (Jeremiah 1:16). Since they refused to honor their Creator and Redeemer, God allowed them to go off into captivity until "the land had enjoyed her Sabbaths" (2 Chronicles 36:21).

The instrument of God's judgment was none other than Babylon itself, the center of sun worship: "Now I have given all these lands into the hand of Nebuchadnezzer king of Babylon, *My servant*" (Jeremiah 27:6, emphasis supplied).

Imagine! God employed Babylon—the archenemy of His truth—as His servant to bring judgment upon His people. Faithful ones like Daniel suffered captivity with the unfaithful. Finally Babylon, still gloating in its triumph, was overthrown so God's remnant could go free:

I shall punish Bel in Babylon, and I shall make what he has swallowed come out of his mouth; and the nations will no longer stream to him. Even the wall of Babylon has fallen down! Come forth from her midst, My people, and each of you save yourselves from the fierce anger of the Lord (Jeremiah 51:44, 45, NASB).

After returning to Jerusalem from captivity in Babylon, God's people learned their lesson about permissive paganism. Unfortunately, they went to the other extreme and lapsed into terrible legalism. "His own received Him not," refusing to come to Him and rest. It's interesting that the first mention in the Gospels of putting Jesus to death appears after a dispute over Sabbath rest (see Mark 3:3-6).

The religious establishment became ever more deeply threatened by Christ's message and His miracles. They outlawed Him and persecuted His followers (see John 9:22). Finally the national council took action to kill the Lord of the Sabbath.

This death decree emerged from a religious coalition against Sabbath rest spearheaded by conservatives, the Pharisees. They united with their rivals, the liberal Sadducees, to join hands with political activitists, the Herodians. They determined that one man ought to die lest the whole nation perish.

This league of apostate clergymen inspired the mob to cry "Crucify Him!" Civil authorities yielded to the popular demand for a death decree, and by this, Pilate and Herod became friends. So in both the religious and political arenas, rival elements achieved an uncommon unity in condemning Jesus.

We must not overlook the role played by a false brother who allied himself with the enemies of Christ. Judas had been a leader among the disciples, but he grew increasingly disillusioned by spiritual developments within the movement. The climax came when he objected to Mary Magdalene's lavish gift of perfume for Jesus. Stung by Christ's rebuke, Judas secretly betrayed his Lord into the hands of the authorities.

After Calvary, Christ's followers suffered a time of trouble and uncertainty when they hid behind locked doors, fearing for their lives. But then came the miracle of Pentecost to bless the church and accelerate its growth.

The earliest Christians were mostly faithful to the gospel. Unfortunately, after the apostles died, apostasy undermined pure faith. Pagan rites and ceremonies infiltrated Christianity.

Not surprisingly, amid such abounding legalism, the day of the sun replaced Sabbath rest.

Spirituality spiraled downward to such depths that the church became Babylon reborn. Reformers led the way out of those dark centuries, but in recent years Protestantism has been lapsing into legalism. Evidence of this is the present move to mingle church and state for the purpose of enforcing religion upon society. Many Protestants have begun to stretch their hands across the gulf to join with Catholics in compelling the country to come back to God.

The Bible warned about religious oppression in the name of God's law. Paul observed that the persecuting son of the flesh comes from Mount Sinai (see Galatians 4:24-31). In a backlash against atheism and the lawless decay of society, Babylon will seek to exterminate those who shun its legalism.

We see a scenario developing remarkably similar to what happened in the first century. Let's recall the end-time events of Christ's life:

- A move arose to save the nation through religious repression, with the focal point of controversy being Sabbath rest.
- Conservatives spearheaded the proceedings, uniting on common ground with liberals and linking up with political activists.
- The unified religious leaders mobilized the people to cry, "Crucify Him!"
- The government yielded to the popular demand for a death decree.
- A false disciple betrayed Jesus into the hands of the authorities.
- During this time of trouble, truehearted disciples grew in their love and unity until the mighty outpouring of Pentecost empowered their message and accelerated their movement.

These circumstances prepared the early church to receive the early rain. We don't need much insight to note similarities with our own situation as we look for the latter rain.

Now, notice another compelling parallel with our time, this one from the Old Testament:

- God sent prophetic warnings for His backslidden people to repent and enter Sabbath rest.
- They refused to respond, so God commissioned Babylon as His servant to bring judgment. The faithful suffered with the unfaithful as Jerusalem was punished and purified.
- Then God turned the tables on the center of sun worship. He called His faithful remnant out of Babylon and blessed them with spiritual prosperity.

Can you see the similarity between Old Testament times and the crisis developing today? Just as God's people back then had backslidden spiritually, so the church today has become lukewarm Laodicea. We've been expecting an attack from Babylon—will God use persecution from the archenemy of truth for the shaking and sifting of His people?

Perhaps this explains the purpose of the Sunday law. *What better way to single out sabbatarians for punishment and purifying than with a Sunday law?*

Something to consider carefully.

The time sequence of this scenario is crucial. *Before* Babylon comes due for its own punishment, God employs that wicked power to punish and purify His people.

But note this: *At no time does Revelation say that Jerusalem becomes Babylon.* God only *uses* Babylon.

God only employs Babylon for our shaking and sifting. The faithful, like Daniel of old, will suffer with the unfaithful during this tribulation. Then God rescues His people out of Babylon and punishes rebellious unbelievers with the seven last plagues.

Adventists have always recognized that God's last-day call to come out of Babylon was prefigured in the Old Testament experience of His people. *What we seem to have overlooked is that God employed Babylon to purify and punish His people.* Understanding this provides new insight into final events.

You see, I used to be sure that Laodicea will finally repent and wake up to spread the three angels' messages. Now I wonder whether things will basically get worse and worse until God finally decides He has seen enough of both our permissiveness and our legalism. Will He once again employ Babylon to punish and purify His people? Is this the real purpose of allowing the Sunday law?

Consider Christian history—persecution has always worked to spread the gospel. Similarly, during the Sunday law crisis, faithless sabbatarians will be punished. Faithful Christians will be purified. The world will be enlightened with God's truth, and the remnant will emerge out of the ruins of persecution. Then probation will close, and Babylon itself will be punished with the plagues. At last Jesus will come!

It's all going to happen sooner than we might expect. Even now in our church, the wheat and the tares are ripening into the harvest. Faithful ones, like Daniel and Mary Magdalene of old, are growing spiritually, while false brethren, like Judas, are confirming themselves in those twin traps of permissiveness or legalism. The stage is being set for a time of trouble from Babylon. A distressing situation awaits our church: "Israel is a scattered flock, the lions have driven them away" (Jeremiah 50:17, NASB).

But praise the Lord for what follows:

> Thus says the Lord of hosts, . . . "Behold, I am going to punish the king of Babylon and his land, . . . and I shall bring Israel back to his pasture . . . . In those days and at that time,' declares the Lord, 'search will be made for the iniquity of Israel, but there will be none; and for the sins of Judah, but they will not be found; for I shall pardon those whom I leave as a remnant" (Jeremiah 50:18-20, NASB).

No room here for lukewarmness or legalism with the remnant. Nothing but loyal trust and obedience.

The challenge for us today is to live and learn and grow. We must rekindle the spirit of the Millerite movement, the spirit

of the Reformation—the willingness to keep on the forward edge of marching truth. Notice this compelling statement from Ellen White:

> No one must be permitted to close the avenues whereby the light of truth shall come to the people. As soon as this shall be attempted, God's Spirit will be quenched, for *that Spirit is constantly at work to give fresh and increased light to His people through His Word.*[2]

Fascinating thought—God is always seeking to reveal new light through His Word. If Ellen White were alive today, she would be as eager as ever to exchange entrenched interpretations for new light. The grand old pillars always remain the same, such as the Sabbath and the 1844 judgment, but we must grow in our understanding of them.

Here in the 1990s, the Seventh-day Adventist Church desperately needs relevance in its prophetic proclamation. Intelligent minds need to be given more than the 1755 Lisbon earthquake as a sign of the times. We need to explain how the fall of Communism is preparing the way for the Sunday law and how Islam may trigger that movement.

I am preparing a follow-up book to this one, entitled *More Hot Potatoes*. It will deal with prophetic relevance plus other hot issues we couldn't take out of the oven this time around. Top of my list of possible topics are:

- Has the Adventist Health System lost its way of worldliness?
- What about our educational system?
- What role should women play in church ministry?
- How can we apply Christian standards regarding divorce and remarriage with compassion?
- Is biblical perfection merely the purging of pickles and peppers?
- Are independent ministries God's designated vehicles to finish the work?

- Since Jesus was "tempted like as we are," does that mean He suffered our sinful passions?
- Why are not more Adventists miraculously healed? Are we missing out on faith healing?

We will dissect other items of controversy as well. Keep in mind that everything you read in these books represents my personal convictions, although I do counsel widely with pastors, church leaders, and laypeople around North America.

Many Adventists become nervous when controversial subjects are put on the table for discussion. I remind them that truth can stand the test of scrutiny. God intends that our proclamation of truth be based upon research, not rehash.

Don't you think so? Ellen White did, and that certainly means something to every conscientious Adventist.

Before we close the pages of this book, let's ponder the parable of the prodigal son. Did you ever notice the context of that story in Luke 15? Christ really targeted His famous parable toward the Pharisees. They represented the prodigal son whom we normally overlook—the intolerant legalist. He was lost too, not in a far-off land of sin, but lost in his works in the father's fields.

When his repenting brother came home from the hogs, bankrupt in self-respect, riches, and righteousness, the happy father staged a celebration:

"Bring out the best robe and put it on him, and put a ring on his hand and sandals on his feet. And bring the fatted calf here and kill it, and let us eat and be merry; for this son of mine was dead and is alive again; he was lost and is found." And they began to be merry (Luke 15:22-24).

As always, someone took offense at the celebration of salvation: "His older son was in the field. And as he came and drew near to the house, he heard music and dancing." "But he was angry and would not go in" (verses 25, 28).

How sad. The angry brother was so bound up by his own works that he couldn't come to the celebration. He was unable to rejoice in his father's mercy. That stubborn refusal to join the celebration of salvation was ominous—there is nothing but damnation in the darkness outside the banquet hall of grace.

Outside our church, in Babylon, God has millions of true-hearted saints with whom He is working wonderfully. For more than a century He has been waiting to bring His people into the fold of truth over which we Adventists have been stewards. Tragically, our church has not been ready to welcome them. Why should God work a miracle now in bringing us a harvest of new members if we are not ready to receive and nurture them—if Khomeini Christians would only hold them hostage?

Let us entrust all this to God's hands as we redouble our efforts for souls to be saved. Soon the Lord will cleanse our camp of both legalism and permissiveness. After He sets His house in order, multitudes of fellow Christians will welcome our Christ-centered truth. Faithful Adventists, joined by these refugees from Babylon, will then comprise the remnant.

At last the mighty Loud Cry will go forth to the ends of the earth, and then shall the end come. Thank God Almighty, we will be home at last.

---

1. Quoted in LeRoy E. Froom, *Movement of Destiny* (Washington, D.C.: Review and Herald, 1971), p. 255, emphasis supplied.

2. *Ibid.*, p. 233.